"*101 Tips* should become every salesperson's cor[...] to respond in a time of need. This perceptive bool[...] tions will guide the newly trained salesperson as w[...] As a compendium of sales solutions, it will help all to see things more clearly.

A broken twig or a shift in the wind may mean little to the untrained hunter who sees it in a forest, but it means a great deal to the trained hunter who perceives its meaning. The accomplished hunter may eventually call this perception common sense but it is far from common knowledge to the untrained hunter who can't wait to learn the secrets. Good hunting will come to those who have the good fortune to learn from Linda Richardson's new book *101 Tips.*"

John P. Conde
Vice President, Marketing
Manufacturers Hanover Trust Company

"New and experienced calling officers will recognize themselves or their fears in many of the examples, and the recommended 'outs' will serve as a good measure where each reader is in his or her development as an effective and natural salesperson. *101 Tips* could be used as a basic teaching text, reference book, or interim refresher guide. In any case, it is full of practical and proven ways to use the sales tips to create sales opportunities."

Ms. Rosemarie B. Greco
Executive Vice President
Fidelity Bank

"Undoubtedly, *101 Tips* is worthwhile reading for both the experienced and inexperienced salesperson who is trusted with generating new business. It is perhaps even more important for the experienced professional who needs to be reminded of the fundamental 'traps' into which he/she may have slipped. Having been reminded myself of my common mistakes, I passed *101 Tips* along to my daughter, who just started a sales career."

Allan F. Munro
Partner
Greenwich Associates

Tips deserves a sub-title: "Everything You Always Wanted to Know about Selling— But Were Afraid to Ask." Richardson has rendered the art of selling a much needed service by distilling the collective experience of effective sales people into a clear, concise and sensitive reference, particularly for bankers new at the selling role. "Old hands" will get some timely pointers for skills developed over the years.

Robert Marino
Vice President, Morgan Guaranty Trust Company

101 TIPS
FOR SELLING
FINANCIAL
SERVICES

101 TIPS
FOR SELLING
FINANCIAL
SERVICES

Linda Richardson

John Wiley & Sons
New York • Chichester • Brisbane • Toronto • Singapore

Library of Congress Cataloging-in-Publication Data:

Richardson, Linda

101 tips for selling financial services.

1. Bank marketing. 2. Selling. I. Title. II. Title:
One hundred and one tips for selling financial services.

HG1616.M3R52   1985   332.1′068   85-22705
ISBN 0-471-83457-2

Printed in the United States of America

10 9 8 7 6 5 4 3 2 1

For Paul

ACKNOWLEDGMENTS

I wish to thank all of the true professionals with whom I have had the privilege of working. Their openness in discussing—and working on—both their sales successes and misses has helped me understand what it is that successful salespeople do that makes them so effective. Their push to keep ahead resulted in developing each of the 101 tips, one by one; their drive for achievement helped close would-be sales traps, and turn them into opportunities for profit and success.

It would be impossible to name all of the outstanding sales professionals whose intuition, experience, and expertise developed these 101 tips. I wish to thank all of our sales training seminar participants for their efforts and insights. Their managers also deserve thanks for their direction along the way. Most important, I thank our client decision-makers for giving me the challenge of selling to them and the privilege of working with their sales forces.

L.R.

CONTENTS

CONTENTS ARRANGED
BY SUBJECT

There are several ways to work with this book. You can use the alphabetical listing in the table of contents to look up individual sales tips. You can use this alternative table of contents by subject as a training guide to improve performance by focusing on specific sales aspects. This table of contents can be used as a self-assessment checklist: Identify key areas that need improvement and work on them first.

101 TIPS
FOR SELLING
FINANCIAL
SERVICES

INTRODUCTION

If you sell "long and hard" you will eventually discover these 101 tips for yourself. However, if you want to avoid learning them the long and hard way and accelerate experience, or if you simply want to revisit the good habits you might have let slide, you will find these 101 tips a helpful guide for sales success *now*. These tips will alert you to the potential traps that lurk within each sale and help you turn every trap into an opportunity for sales success.

101 Tips looks at 101 common sales situations — situations that can become opportunities or traps — it's up to you. Their cumulative effect may prove to be enough to win or lose a piece of business or a long term sales relationship.

These tips have been written to help point your way through situations as sensitive as PRICE OBJECTIONS (what do you say to "Your competitor has offered it to me for a lower fee"?), or as seemingly harmless as SEATING (given a choice, is it better to sit directly across from a customer or at a right angle?). Arranged alphabetically, these situations — and 99 others — can be looked up in advance of a sale, *before* you let them become traps.

I would like to note, however, that there is a risk in presenting these 101 tips as individual issues. It is not just the BUSINESS CARDS, CLOSING, COFFEE, SEATING, and so on that make the critical difference, but it is the appropriate blend of correct habits involving these that tells the customer *you* are the professional to do business with.

The objective in learning these tips is to assimilate them, not to memorize them. The purpose is not to create an overly analytical, awkward salesperson who worries about minding

1

each P and Q but to develop effective, natural salespeople who have good selling habits. Consider each tip presented in this book as one piece of a puzzle. As with a puzzle, the more pieces you have, the greater the opportunity to create a total picture. Although some people may have more of the pieces of the puzzle intuitively and can use them instinctively, the real key to sales success is being prepared with as many pieces as possible, and trusting yourself to put them to work.

Take a look at these 101 tips. You may be able to turn one of them into an opportunity—today.

ASKING FOR THE BUSINESS (CLOSING)

There are many stories of how salespeople won deals because they asked for the business. One banker who habitually asks, "What else can I do today for you?" as a second close for his calls left a luncheon with a $50 million loan. But what about those who lost opportunities because they *didn't ask*? Another banker who neglected to ask for the business at the end of a sales interview did not get it. The customer later said, "He never did ask for the business, *so I didn't give it to him*." That $1 million loan went to a competitor.

Many salespeople are reluctant to ask outright for their customer's business. Like most people they do not want to be rejected. But there are ways to reduce this risk. By asking questions to get customer feedback throughout the sales interview (see CLOSING INCREMENTALLY/CHECKING), you will be able to predict with some certainty what your customer's response to your close will be. Positive feedback from the customer will give you the information and confidence you need to *ask for the business*.

In selling financial services, closing often entails a series of interim steps that leads to the sale. Closing at the *end of each call* is essential whether the close is "sign on the dotted line" or "take the first step" in a series of steps. Without asking questions like "When can you send me a copy of your portfolio so that I can determine . . . and call you to discuss . . .?" to achieve your first step, you may never get to your final action step close: "When can we transfer the funds so that yoú can begin to earn the additional interest?"

In some cases the close is initiated by the customer who asks, "How do I get started?" However, in most situations, if

3

you don't ask for the business it is *very unlikely* that you will get it. And at times just asking is not enough. You have to follow up and give an extra special effort, such as more frequent contacts, flying in several times, bringing in senior management, or organizing a special *presentation. Whenever there is an indication of interest, you should ask for the business in a direct and confident way.* Each sales contact should conclude with your asking for the order or getting agreement on what the next step will be.

Asking for the business is what selling is *all* about. Closing begins *before* you meet with the customer—when you set your sales call objective. It permeates the entire sales call as you close incrementally to find out how things are progressing, and it wraps up the sales interview when you find out what the customer wants to do. One division executive, renowned for his deal-making, always asks his people, "How many pens do you have?" before they go on their sales calls to remind them just why they are going out. Remember to *ask for the business, look for it, and be aware of it.* Your customers expect you to close and are bewildered when you don't.

(See CLOSING INCREMENTALLY/CHECKING, OBJECTIVES FOR SALES CALL, NEXT STEP, and FOLLOW-UP.)

BODY LANGUAGE

Although all body gestures are subject to different interpretations, there are a number of gestures in selling situations that will more often than not provide you with additional insight and information concerning the customer's thinking. Awareness and recognition of these gestures can be very useful to you in reading customers and adjusting your approach. Some typical gestures include folding arms across the chest (closed off), crossing legs away from the salesperson (responding negatively, guarded), rubbing one's nose (not pleased, you "struck a nerve"), clasping hands behind the head (disengaging, the meeting is ending/ended for all intents and purposes!), fiddling with a chain or paper clip (nervousness or tension), poising hands in a steeple (pontificating, "I'm an expert on this"), glancing down quickly ("It's my turn to talk"), doodling ("Give me attention," "Let me talk"), not looking at you for an extended period (customer stopped listening), nodding head up and down and turning body toward seller (positive, interested). Your ability to read these and other gestures can add to your understanding of the customer.

The following example illustrates how "reading" body signals provided insight for one salesperson. As an account manager described a particular feature and benefit of his product, he observed his customer move her back slightly deeper into her chair, quickly stretch her neck upward, and look upward for a split second. He "read" this as a negative response to what he said. The account manager tested his suspicion by saying, "It looks as if this isn't sitting well with you, Mary. May I ask if I am off in how I'm approaching this?" In so doing he was able to test the message in a nonthreatening way. His customer confirmed his observation stating, "That's not at all what I want. We've had numerous . . .; none have worked. I can't repeat what we have already tried. What I'm looking for is . . . ." By observing and testing the nonverbal signal, the account manager was able to adjust his approach and move in sync with the customer's needs and concerns.

As this example shows, *body language should supplement, not replace, verbal feedback.* Since gestures may be habitual or coincidental, all nonverbal messages should be tested before being acted on. As you think about body language, check out your own gestures to make sure they do not impede what you say by giving off unintentional messages.

BUSINESS CARDS

Business cards are an important part of customer contact. Depending on the situation or the relationship, cards can be used in a variety of ways: presenting your card to new customers at the beginning of the sales interview, offering your card at the conclusion of the interview, sending your card with a follow-up letter, presenting your card to the secretaries as well as customers, and so forth. Giving a card to a prospect at the outset helps the prospect remember your name during the call, and clipping your card to a brochure or article personalizes it.

In all situations, you should have your cards handy in your suit or shirt pocket or in a card case. Avoid ever having to rummage for your cards. Never say, "Well, I have one somewhere. Just let me look . . . ." Although it is always preferable to have a fresh, crisp card on hand, if a customer asks for your card and you do not have one (you are new to the organization, etc.), simply say nondefensively that you do not have a card but will send one to the customer. Refrain from giving a long explanation, and be sure to follow up and send the customer a card. Also remember to get cards from your customer (when appropriate) to ensure that you have his or her correct title and spelling. When a card is presented to you *look* at the card for a second (the title may surprise you), look at the customer, and say thank you. Immediately put the card away. Otherwise you might leave it on the customer's desk!

To show the importance of being prepared with cards, a senior vice-president candidly recounted an embarrassing situation to entry level salespeople in his division. It seems he did not have a card at an important luncheon with his executive vice-president and the CEO of a priority relationship. His embarrassment was magnified because his EVP had specifically asked him to give a card to the customer. The senior vice-president said that at his level this oversight was *inexcusable*; as a senior vice-president, he was expected to set standards of professional excellence. He used this example to illustrate that professionalism starts with the smallest detail.

CARING

Your attitude about the customer is probably the most important factor in determining how effective you are with customers and how productive you are for your organization and yourself. A genuinely caring attitude shines through and can be contagious. Such an attitude stems from the respect you have for yourself, your institution, and your customer. It is an internal voice which makes preparation, value added, follow-up, enthusiasm, and honesty the underlying values that drive your performance. Caring reflects the high level of importance you place on each and every customer, and is the keystone, whether he or she is with a Fortune 100 company or a mom-and-pop store. It can be verbalized by a statement such as, "Remember, Mike, I'm part of the package in service, and if there is a problem call me . . . ."

Caring can be seen in the quality of service customers receive. It is more than what you say; it is what you do, and it is often paid for by customer loyalty. All people want to feel important and this is especially true in a buy/sell relationship. Customers are happy to do business with salespeople whom they proudly describe as *MY* account executive, *MY* banker, or *MY* broker. Remember, people buy from people, not from institutions, and (in basically competitive situations) nothing is more important than *you* in determining whether or not the customer does business with you. (See RAPPORT, RELATING.)

CLOSING INCREMENTALLY/ CHECKING

All salespeople are interested in improving their ability to close. Many salespeople shy away from closing because they don't want to bear the discomfort of selling's most negative experience: rejection.

The incremental close is a process you can use to circumvent or even avoid rejection. By gathering customer feedback *throughout* the interview, you can reduce the risk associated with closing. Incremental closing (checking) consists of questioning the customer *during* the sales interview to get direct feedback on how you are doing with the sale. With this information you can predict how your customer will respond to your close (request for action), and be more confident in asking for the business at the *right time*.

Make it a point to close incrementally when you have responded to an objection or presented a key feature and benefit ("How does our 24-hour turnaround compare?" or simply "How does that sound to you?") so that you can get *direct customer feedback*. The sum total of this incremental feedback will help you predict how the customer will react to your close. Too often salespeople confuse customer silence with agreement; the incremental close will help you avoid this costly mistake.

The benefits of closing incrementally *throughout* the interview are numerous: it will let you know if *an objection or issue has or has not been resolved* to the customer's satisfaction. If a customer says, "I'm still concerned about . . ." you will know that you probably have to cover more ground on the subject. It will also tell you when it is *appropriate to move on to another point* because you have satisfied the customer's objection. The incremental close can lead the customer to close ("How can I get started?"). It can also tell you when *not to ask for the business* because your customer's reactions are overwhelmingly negative. When this occurs you can say, "At this time this does not look like the deal for you." Candor on your part, when both you and the customer know the customer is not interested, will be respected by most customers and will increase your credibility. This respect and acknowledgment of negative customer reactions can save valuable time for you and your customer and can sometimes open up new opportunities.

The incremental close will help you with customers who, in spite of their positive responses during the call, reject your close or refuse to take the next logical step at the conclusion of the call. You can use the points of agreement as grounds to inquire about their reluctance to act. You can say, "Tom, since we've discussed the . . . and how it could save . . . . may I ask what concerns you have about starting now to . . .?" In this way you may be able to uncover what is troubling the customer.

But most importantly, the incremental close will give you the confidence to close. Closing incrementally helps you know where you are, what to do, what to fix, and when it is appropriate to close. It gives you the information and confidence you need to ask for the business. [See ASKING FOR THE BUSINESS (CLOSING).]

COFFEE

Yes, it is a good idea to accept an invitation from your customer to have coffee, even if it's just a half cup (for health reasons, etc.). Not only is the acceptance of hospitality common courtesy, but it can also create a first connection. Moreover, as one successful senior executive puts it, "At the very least the coffee guarantees me a certain amount of time in the office." However, be considerate and take cues from the customer as to whether or not he or she is having coffee or if it is convenient to serve coffee (if the customer will have to send out for it, etc.). If you only drink decaffeinated coffee or herbal teas and neither is available, simply say, "No, thank you." If you do accept coffee *drink it*, and if you are just starting out, take care not to spill it.

COMPETITIVE INFORMATION FROM CUSTOMERS

Customers are a great source of competitive information. Therefore it is important to know how to gather information from them, assess its validity, and use it to your advantage. If, for example, a customer mentions a competitor, you should be alert to a possible competitive threat. Find out as much as you can about the competitor without showing signs of being overly concerned or rattled. Since your objective is to determine how real the threat is, you should calmly question such things as: Who is the competitor? What is in the offer? What is the price? What are the time frames? How does the customer feel about the competitor? and What is the customer's experience with the competitor? This should be done tactfully by explaining that this kind of information *will help you and the customer compare value and look at the alternatives side by side.* Most customers will share some information with you when they think they can benefit from it. How much they share usually depends on their comfort, confidence, and trust in you, and in your ability to convey that you are trying to help.

If the customer refuses to provide you with information, do not take it personally. Remember, he or she is not obliged to give you this information. Some customers may think it is just not cricket. Others who decline to share information about competitors with you may be responding to *how* you asked, rather than what you asked. You may have forgotten the golden rule of sales: "Give before you get!" or you might have failed to tell the customer why you are asking (to help him or her make a comparison since no two deals are exactly alike). Other customers may be using the "competition" as a negotiating ploy and this will enable you to *test* whether the competitive offer is real or just a ploy. Such information will help you withstand the pressure and help you preserve your price or terms. Even when a customer makes no mention of a competitor, you should check to find out who else may be in the picture.

When you do succeed in getting competitive information from customers, you should use it to position your offer and help the customer compare total deals. Remember, rarely are two products/deals exactly alike; make sure the customer and you know what the true differences are, always comparing apples with apples by considering total value. (See CRITICIZING THE COMPETITION and OFFSETTING COMPETITORS.)

COMPETITIVE INTELLIGENCE

All the competitive intelligence that you gather from the customer during sales interviews, or from the "street," should be channeled back to your organization. Your line feedback, ideas, and experiences are *invaluable* in keeping your organization competitive since it is you, as the line salesperson, who has greatest access to competitive data via customers. Regardless of whether the competitive data is hearsay or fact, it is important to your organization. Hearsay and rumors must be substantiated or squelched to ensure that they do not hurt morale or misdirect internal efforts ("X has a lower fee," when in fact it does not).

Gathering and sharing competitive information is one of the best ways to be prepared to offset the competition and help your organization remain competitive. Don't waste the precious competitive information you have griping over coffee. Communicate such data to the area of your institution where it can be verified, shared with the salesforce, and used to improve products and marketing strategies.

If a customer gives you feedback about your own company which is inaccurate or malicious, it is important to tell the customer that you appreciate his or her candor. You should try to get specific information about the rumor, impression, and source. Once you have the information, take the time to address it in a nondefensive way, and to dispel the negative information. When you return to your institution, be sure to communicate the information to your manager.

COMPETITIVE PRESENTATIONS

Find out when competitors are making their presentations. It can be helpful to be the *last presentor*, since your competitor will have either educated or confused your customer for you by the time you make your sales call. In either case coming last works to your advantage, since it will enable you to clarify any points of confusion, respond to more specific questions, and make the final impression. In most situations, depending on the relationship and customer, before you make your presentation you can ask how the competitor's presentation went and what issues were raised. You can gain valuable insights that you can use in planning your presentation.

When you do present, make sure you are fully prepared (practice), and that your materials are well organized, tailored to the customer, and packaged in a crisp, professional way. Be sure you have a sufficient quantity of proposals, and materials for the customers who will attend. When you are in a competitive situation it is very important toward the end of your presentation to ask, *"What concerns/problems are there that we have not covered?"* Be *quiet* after you ask this question and look at your customer, keeping your head straight (tilted head says "be easy on me"). The idea is to unearth concerns *when you are there* so that you have the opportunity to satisfy them.

Remember to explicitly express your interest in getting the business, and state your commitment to delivering a quality product. In competitive situations *be keenly aware of the customer's decision time frames* and *increase frequency of contact* (personal visits and telephone calls) with him or her as the decision deadline approaches. One banker telephoned the customer the next day to follow up on his presentation.

16

When he asked the customer how she thought it went, she said, "It went fairly well, BUT . . ." and proceeded to describe her company's concern regarding his bank's technical/operations staff. The banker arranged a joint call with one of his technical people and during the call was able to allay this concern by demonstrating the bank's professionalism and state-of-the-art technology. Remember, when customers are about to make a decision, it is important for you to know what they need and to be there to provide it.

CONTROL

Salespeople frequently express concern over loss of control during a sales interview. What does loss of control really mean? It means that the customer is the one who is driving the interview. But the salesperson should control the sales call because he or she is the one responsible for orchestrating a meaningful sales dialogue. Control is a way to provide direction for a sales call, not to monopolize it. One important way customers take control is by taking control of the questions, thereby determining when, what and how subjects are covered. But you, too, can use questions to regain control.

Questions can help you regain control not only with aggressive customers who confront you with a barrage of objections, questions, or complaints, but also with less aggressive customers. Questions can help you *set* the direction of the dialogue rather than just respond to it. With aggressive customers, questions can change your defense to an offense. For example, when your customer says, "And furthermore, I'm concerned about the legal aspects in offshore investing," you can demonstrate your confidence by asking for more information about the concern rather than immediately trying to answer the objection. You can begin to direct the discussion by asking, "Yes, that's understandable. What specific concern do you have about the legality so that I can focus on . . .?" By seeking more information you can be the one to direct, focus, and subtly regain control. Inexperienced salespeople might think that asking such questions of a hard charging customer would only make things worse; however, questioning and listening is the first step in showing confidence and regaining control.

Another way to use questions as a control technique is to

help pace a customer who is all over the place, jumping from topic to topic. Unless you can control this type of customer, you are apt to find that you cover a lot of ground without resolving anything. With a customer who jumps from topic to topic, you should conclude each key statement you make with a question, thereby obliging the customer to respond to what you have said rather than letting him or her jump to another point without achieving closure on the one at hand. For example, after you have explained to your customer that the training for the new system would take one day, you could close incrementally by asking, "So how would Ron's spending the day with Sue from our operations area for one day to . . . work out for you?" and then ask, "When should we schedule . . . ?" In this way you would know where you stand on the training requirement before moving on to a new point. If you find that the discussion has gotten sidetracked anyway, questions can also help you get back on track. There really isn't anything wrong with going off on tangents providing you know *how* and *when to get back*.

The objective of using questions is to create a *balanced sales dialogue* which is orchestrated by you, the salesperson. While the word control sometimes has negative connotations, it is used here in a positive way to mean "lead" the sales interview. It is the responsibility of the salesperson to be prepared for the call and to focus the discussion. Control means *never* losing sight of your objectives, and questions are an excellent tool for keeping everyone on track and achieving objectives.

CREDIBILITY

Credibility is a must. Whether it is follow-up, service, or delivery, customers must be able to count on you and trust in what you say. If you are asked a question and you don't know the answer, *don't fake it. It is better to lose a sale than to risk losing your credibility.* Tell the customer you will look into the question and arrange a time to get back to him or her with the information. Be honest, not apologetic or defensive. Don't give a convoluted explanation about why you don't know, such as, "I really wouldn't feel comfortable talking about that, since I am in *X* group and we do . . . but we have . . . ." It is better to say something like "That's something I'd like to look into," or "That's a highly specialized area . . . . We have specialists who . . . . I can arrange . . . ."

After you say that you'd like to look into "*X*" further, you can say, "May I ask *what prompts the question* so that I can understand . . . ?" This will provide you with insight into what the customer really wants to know, how interested the customer really is, and what plans and so forth the question may be related to. It will also help you reestablish a balance by showing you are not "thrown" by a question you cannot answer. A question which is out of your depth might also be the perfect opportunity to arrange an appointment for the specialist (make sure the customer qualifies!). But under no circumstances put your credibility at risk by inventing an answer to a question.

Maintaining your credibility is equally important when dealing within your organization. If you are presenting to your credit committee, for example, and someone in your institution asks you, "Who's on their board?" and you don't know, respond with, "I'll look into that and get back to you . . . ."

20

While having a particular piece of information is better than the infamous "I'll get back to you," a sincere statement that you will in fact get back to them—and then following up—is your best bet. (See FOLLOW-UP.)

CRITICIZING THE COMPETITION

Never make derogatory comments about your competitors. Negative remarks about competitors actually boost and legitimize them, and can cause you to be perceived as petty or unprofessional. Although it is *unprofessional* to attack competitors in front of customers, *it is important to know how to emphasize your competitive advantages in a professional way to offset the competition. By using questions you can help both you and your customer make comparisons based on the differences that exist.* For example, if you as a banker are competing with a broker, you could ask the customer about his or her experience with the broker/institution. Never directly attack the competition by saying, for example, "They are transaction-oriented (churn) and we are relationship-oriented." Rather, take a few minutes to find out the customer's experience with the competitor, ask a question that will point out your competitor's weakness, discuss your approach. In this way you can find out what you are up against, avoid offending the customer (who may have known the broker for 10 years), and make specific comparisons. Similarly, if you are competing with an organization that has recently undergone a series of management or policy changes and is now trying to get to your customer by underbidding, do not directly criticize its revolving door senior management and fair weather policies. Instead ask, "What has been your experience with them?" and then discuss your consistency in the middle market, and how this consistency in policy and management ensures that you will be there in the future. With your help your customer will compare and recognize the advantage of working with you.

CROSS-SELLING

There is no question that providing comprehensive services increases ease, convenience, and savings for customers. It can also increase profitability for your institution. For these reasons "relationship building" has become important to most financial services today.

Cross-selling of services to present customers to maintain and expand relationships has become a critical objective in financial services marketing. It is mutually advantageous because it helps tie customers to you, making it harder for them to leave, yet it also benefits customers by giving them convenience and negotiation leverage. Cross-selling is one of the best ways to strengthen a relationship. You should always ask questions to find out *what else* your customers need even if it is outside your area, such as an answer to a trade question.

Of course you cannot maximize cross-sell opportunities without product knowledge of the full range of financial products which your organization offers and your customers use. The time you take to develop some in-depth knowledge of the products and how they can meet your customers' needs is well worth the effort. You do not have to become a specialist in each product, but if you are to successfully *initiate* opportunities you do need to know more than the name of the specialist and a telephone number. Since cross-selling calls for teamwork it is important for you to develop good working relationships with product areas or specialists in order to have access to them and their resources.

As important as having the broad product knowledge to satisfy the full spectrum of customer needs is a PROACTIVE and persistent sales attitude of order-maker, not order-taker.

Remember that you are a part of your institution, not just your division. The most successful salespeople are generally the best promoters of this multiproduct sales approach because they know that ultimately it means all-around stronger and more profitable customer relationships. (See PRODUCT KNOWLEDGE and NETWORKING IN YOUR OWN ORGANIZATION.)

CUSTOMER CRISIS
(POSTPONING SALES CALL)

As you arrive for your appointment, you discover that your customer is in the midst of a crisis and has to cut the meeting short (shows that he or she is disturbed, visually distracted, or mentions a pressing problem to you). First, emphathize with the customer about the problem ("*Sorry to hear that . . .*") and, if appropriate, ask if there is anything you can do. If you have a close relationship with the customer offer a sympathetic ear or shoulder.

When the crisis is business related, *look for ways to turn the problem into a sales or problem-solving opportunity.*

If the customer is disturbed and you cannot be of help, quickly *volunteer* to postpone your meeting, even if it means getting back on an airplane (perhaps you can meet with someone else while you are there). This will work to your advantage in the long run, since customers will appreciate your consideration and judgment.

Under no circumstances should you take your customer's action personally.

One salesperson found an excellent opportunity through his empathy and sensitivity to a customer's problem. During the sales call, the customer became visibly disturbed by a telephone message. After receiving the message from his secretary the customer said, "Oh, I *can't stand* to get into that now, tell him I'll get back to him." The salesman said, "Would you like some privacy for that now?" The customer began talking about a problem with employees and the discussion led to cross-selling a pension plan.

Customers are people too, and they have concerns and needs as people which you should recognize and respect.

This kind of sensitivity and awareness will help you differentiate yourself from salespeople who cannot see beyond their objectives. [See EMPATHY (RELATING).]

CUSTOMER LEVEL OF KNOWLEDGE

Rather than make assumptions about how knowledgeable or sophisticated your customer is about a particular product or approach, find out what his or her level of sophistication is. If you assume, "They must be familiar with X," or say to the customer, "I'm not sure how familiar you are with X" (and proceed to tell the customer about X without finding out), you are likely to go over or under your customer's head, and waste valuable time. It is much more effective to ask questions such as, "Would it help if I went over the way it works?" or "How familiar are you with the mechanics of . . . ?"

By tactfully asking about a customer's familiarity with the service you are about to discuss you may learn not only how much he or she already knows, but how he or she came to know about it. You may learn that it is one of your competitors who has been educating your customer.

You may also be very surprised to learn that you have overestimated your customer's familiarity with and level of knowledge of the product. For example, after a two and one-half hour presentation on a $750 million deal, the CEO of a major company asked, to the dismay of the team of bankers making the call, "By the way, what is a swap?" While the treasurer fully understood what the bankers were proposing, the CEO most definitely did not. Had they tested their assumptions, this team of bankers, one of whom is exceptional in the field, could have easily built a simple explanation for the mechanics and benefits relative to the customer's situation into the presentation at an early point. Not having done this, the team had to redraft the proposal and make a second call. A mistake like this is costly in time and money, and can jeopardize the business.

Since there are often different levels among customers present in a sales call, it is important to know *who knows what.* Whenever possible you should try to have one-on-one pre-meetings to bring people up to speed and eliminate surprises. You should always be prepared to describe your service in a clear and simple manner.

Remember to test your assumptions about how much your customer knows or does not know and how much he or she needs/wants to know. Unless you test assumptions about levels of knowledge you will risk making presentations that bore, perplex, and waste your time as well as your customer's time.

CUSTOMER NEEDS

Before discussing your service/product capabilities you should have information about two things: (1) *What* the customer is doing *now* and (2) *How* the situation could be *improved.* The gap between the "now" and the "future" represents the window of sales opportunity for you. Unless you know what the customer's situation and needs are, you really cannot satisfy these needs or take advantage of the sales opportunities that exist. Only after you understand the customer's situation, needs and plans, can you present the serv-- ices that will have impact on those needs.

By asking questions to uncover needs you can help customers analyze their own situation. A customer may not even know he or she has a need, but *good questioning* by you can help the customer *self-discover.* For example, for cash management, you could inquire, "How do you presently collect your deposits?" "How beneficial would it be to accelerate the collection to . . . improve cash flow and pay down that loan?" These questions will enable you and the customer to zero in on needs and opportunities and will help you have relevant, personalized sales dialogues with your customers.

As you begin to discuss your services, you should weave the *customer's needs, the customer's situation, the customer's plans, the customer's concerns* and *the customer's examples* into your description. In this way you can *tailor what you say about your products.* Product discussions that are not related *specifically* to the customer (canned pitches) are sterile and usually will not sell.

Keep in mind too that customers have *emotional* as well as business needs. For example, one bank made an acquisition offer. But the target bank refused despite the competitive superiority of the bank's bid and opted instead to go with another offer. The reason: ego—the president of the target bank did not want to leave his office behind.

Too often salespeople rush into discussion of their product or develop a sales strategy that does not take customer needs into account. This is a common but *fatal mistake*. Not knowing needs makes it all but impossible to satisfy them. (See "WHAT DO YOU HAVE FOR ME TODAY?")

CUSTOMER SATISFACTION WITH PRESENT SERVICE

Before exploring new needs or *before introducing a new idea or sensitive subject such as a fee increase*, inquire about the customer's level of satisfaction with the present situation. Ask the customer how the cash management system which was put in place two months ago is working before discussing a new investment module. If there is a problem, understand and solve it prior to introducing a new idea or fee increase. Satisfied customers are much more receptive to increased fees or add-on business.

CUSTOMER'S OFFICE

Be considerate of the customer's "space." Observe courtesies and follow the customer's lead regarding coasters, smoking, and so forth. Many nonsmokers prefer not to be around smokers. Therefore, unless your customer is a smoker and is smoking (or you know the customer very well, if ashtrays are visible, or if you ask), it is usually advisable not to smoke in the customer's office. Likewise be sure to observe your customer's office décor (furniture, pictures, photographs, diplomas, certificates, art, trophies, etc.) to gain insight into your customer's values, style, and approach. These items—when your comments are genuine and well timed—can be effective icebreakers and rapport builders. (See RAPPORT.)

CUSTOMER'S PRESENT SYSTEM—REPLACING IT

You should be tactful in how you suggest improvements and changes, and be alert to the personal dynamics involved. While your objective may be to replace an old system, you should find out as much as possible about the system in place to determine how the change will affect the person you are talking to. Ask, "So that I can understand, what . . .? When was the system put in? . . . Who was involved with that? . . . What aspects might you want altered? . . . improved? . . . What is working?" and "What would you like to see different?"

The customer you are speaking with may be the one who designed the old system and, therefore, may have a stake in its preservation. This person may be threatened by the new system (concerned about a loss of jobs, fewer people to manage, loss of power, or having management look on a change as a poor reflection on his or her own present performance). You should always find out how your customer feels about and fits into the present system. Think twice about how you phrase your analysis, especially if you are in a group situation in which someone could "lose face."

When you are speaking with the system's architect or supporter, do not blatantly criticize it. Rather, discuss *how things have changed* (the person has not done a poor job, X has changed), and how these changes call for modifications. Then present to the customer your new ideas, their capabilities and benefits as designed to meet the new challenges or new objectives, and build on what has already been accomplished or is in place. Whether or not the individual(s) you are selling to has a personal stake in the old system, you should remember that most people fear change; therefore, always be ready to demonstrate specific benefits and give assurances of improvement.

CUSTOMER'S TELEPHONE

Use your charge card number when you have to use your customer's telephone to make long distance calls. Whenever possible, make your telephone calls in a private setting, especially when you are actually trying to solve the customer's problem. A case in point is the banker whose manager hung up on him, leaving him shocked and at a loss for words, while the customer stood next to him.

DECISION-MAKING AUTHORITY

It is essential to understand how decisions are made in your customer's organization. Unfortunately this information is not always readily available. If you directly ask, "Do you have the authority to make this decision?" some customers will feel pressed to say "yes" to protect their status and egos. Thus it is more effective to ask process-oriented questions such as, "May I ask who will be involved in *your* decision process?" or "What are the steps . . . ?" or "How are decisions like this made in your organization?" These questions show the customer that you understand that levels of influence and authority exist in all companies. The customer will feel less defensive and will most likely give you the kind of information you need to plan a successful strategy. (See DECISION-MAKING UNIT.)

DECISION-MAKING UNIT

It is critical for you to find out who will be involved in the decision-making process so that you can identify and satisfy the *buying criteria* of the decision-maker(s) and influencer(s) In the case of more unusual products the company's decision-making unit may cut across departments, functions, and disciplines. You may find yourself meeting with the treasurer, a tax specialist, and a corporate development person, all with different needs, objectives, and buying motives. The key is to find out who's who and to work out a strategy to meet *each one's buying criteria*. Whenever possible it is very useful to meet one-on-one with each decision-maker or influencer to enable you to package a proposal that takes *all needs* into consideration.

When a customer mentions a third party (high — economic decision-maker or wide — influencer) such as the treasurer, an accountant, or a relative, who will be involved in making the decision, be sure to inquire about and try to meet one-on-one with the individuals so that you can influence them favorably toward you. Before you meet with new members of the decision-making unit get as much information as possible. Ask your present contact such questions as, "May I ask how long she's been here?" or "What is his background?" or "How did she feel about the switchover?" so that you do not go into the meeting cold and approach things from the wrong perspective. While you may not get access to all levels of the decision-making group, it does not hurt to ask. A question such as "When would (or Would) it be possible for *us* (do not exclude your present contact) to meet with Joe?" is well worth asking.

In situations where you are blocked from meeting or it is

inappropriate for you to meet or speak with the other decision-maker(s), you should gather as much information as possible from your contact in order to address all concerns in your proposal. When your contact will be the one to make a presentation to the board for you, for example, you should do as much as you can to help prepare your contact ("Would it help if I prepared an outline/proposal . . .?") for the meeting or to make yourself available for questions before or during the presentation. How much information your contact shares with you regarding the real decision-making process and how much access you have to other members of the decision-making group are good indications of the confidence and trust the customer has in you and where you stand.

Be sure to ask about and look at communication patterns in the customer's organization (who speaks to whom, who sends what to whom, who carbon copies whom). Knowing these patterns will help you figure out how decisions are made and who needs to be sold by whom. Make sure you don't ruffle feathers. The key is to understand how the decision-making unit works, and to make contacts to cover all of your bases. (See ELEVATING CONTACT LEVEL.)

DECLINING

Sometimes it is necessary to decline a transaction with a present customer, a referral from a good customer, or a prospective customer. You should be sensitive to the impact that refusal can have on the customer. Declining the deal without leaving the customer feeling hostile and angry with you and your organization should be your objective.

Of course, the best way to decline a transaction is to get the customer to be the one to say, "No." This takes time and skill. For example, when the nephew of the bank's largest private banking customer applied for a loan but did not meet the bank's criteria, the private banker approached the nephew in this way: "We'd be happy to *consider* this, but have you thought through . . .?" By showing the customer the payment terms relative to his cash flow, the banker was able to lead the customer to rethink the prudence of the transaction and decide on his own not to pursue the loan.

Unfortunately, this approach takes a good deal of time and will not always work. In most situations you will have to be the one to say no to the deal. For example, one bank that does not have an appetite for construction loans frequently has to decline this kind of business with its own customers. One of the bankers, who manages to do this very well without alienating her customers, says she does this by knowing the criteria of her bank for exceptions to policy, finding out the basics of the deal to determine if the loan would possibly qualify, getting back to the customer immediately, explaining that no bank does "everything," specifically avoiding the word "policy," discussing alternatives, and, whenever possible, making a referral to another institution that is active in the business (but not likely to take her business). This banker does not abdicate her role simply because she cannot close one particular deal. How you decline makes all the difference.

The following are some guidelines to help you decline in a constructive way:

Be sure you *know the reason* for refusing the transaction, and *explain the reason* in a clear, nondefensive, helpful manner (if you don't know why, *ask* your manager).

Make sure all that could have been done has been done.

Do not procrastinate since unnecessary delay in informing the customer can be more upsetting than not being able to do the deal (no news is good news). Your procrastination may prevent customers from pursuing other options, seeking other alternatives, cancelling orders or getting refunds, and so forth.

Show empathy by saying "no" to the transaction, not the person (use the word "this" rather than "you").

Decline in person at the customer's site rather than over the telephone whenever possible (if, because of time/distance/schedule factors, you find it necessary to decline over the telephone, and if you are interested in future business, set up a follow-up personal appointment during the telephone conversation).

For priority relationships or in very sensitive situations, bring your manager to demonstrate to the customer your organization's concern and interest.

Don't blame others in your organization since, in the long run, siding with the customer against your organization will hurt your credibility. Instead say, "Dan, I looked at this carefully and *did all I could*. At this time because of . . . , *we* can't participate in this deal."

Take ownership for the decision even if you are not fully convinced the decision not to participate is a good one.

Express your differences internally and try to reach an understanding with your management, but do not present your organization as a house divided. Remember, no one has unlimited authority, and as part of a team, you are part of the decision.

Suggest *alternatives* whenever possible and make the contact.

The key to successful declining is to at least satisfy the customer emotionally, if not financially. The objective should be to keep the door open for future deals, not to burn bridges, and not to undermine your own organization.

DINING OUT

Always remember what your business dinner objective is: *to strengthen the customer's relationship* with you and your institution. Sharing a meal is an opportunity to get to know your customer and increase your understanding of the customer and the organization. It is an opportunity to go beyond the level of discussion in a regular business meeting to uncover personal motives, insights into priorities, and more private plans about direction and strategy. It is also the time to learn more personal information about the customer, his or her family, and interests. It could be the time to ask questions that may not be appropriate in an office or to explore an interesting topic that came up that your customer seemed reluctant to pursue with others present. For example, you could say, "Bill, you mentioned Joe might not be handling that," and wait for the customer to expand further on the change. Or it could be the time to ask, "How's it been going . . . your son . . . (more personal matter)?" Remember, rarely should a business dinner be treated like a regular sales call. Most customers do not want to talk straight business after 7:00 P.M.; therefore, handle the occasion, depending on the customer, with a healthy mix of the interpersonal and business.

While you should enjoy your customer and the occasion, it is your customer's enjoyment, not yours, which is most important. Some tips to remember to help keep the customer as the focal point and maximize the opportunity include:

Ask the customer or customer's secretary about a favorite restaurant and book your reservations there.

If you are selecting the restaurant, choose one in which you know the menu and service, and the staff knows you.

42

Arrange for the bill to come to you, presign the check, or use your club card.

Let your guest order first.

Order your meal without much ado (don't over-complicate the ordering of *your* meal: don't ask "How is this . . . ? What is on this . . . ? Could you substitute . . . for . . . ?" etc.).

Let the customer enjoy his or her meal while you talk (this is a great time to sell the relationship, ideas, or in some situations, the benefits of a product, etc.).

Pace your eating with the customer's so that you don't finish 15 minutes before or after he or she does.

Take a cue about ordering drinks from the customer.

Never be the one to raise an unpleasant topic *during* the meal; it's impolite and unhealthy.

Take a cue about when/if to discuss a business subject.

Use your judgment in pacing the conversation and deciding on the business/social ratio (include ample time for chit-chat when you arrive at the restaurant; some salespeople will bring up business only over coffee, if at all).

Use the more personal setting to uncover private information (background, family, aspirations, and plans) from the customer, which will help you know and understand him or her, and which can strengthen the relationship.

Always remember basic manners:

Place your napkin on your lap as soon as you are seated.

Put your knife on the edge of the plate, not the table, after you use it.

Put butter onto your bread plate, not directly on your bread.

Place both your knife and fork parallel at 3 o'clock towards the center of plate, not the edge of the plate, at the end of the meal.

Begin to eat first since you are the host, but wait until *everyone* and *everything* is served.

Give the customer the best seat (view).

Manners are as important in a professional setting as in an interpersonal one!

For group situations, preplan seating so that guests don't have to be concerned about where they should sit. For more formal senior situations use place cards when possible. *Integrate* your colleagues among the customers, plan who will sit next to whom, and place the senior customer to the right of your most senior person. (See ENTERTAINMENT.)

DRESS

Look to the successful managers you admire in your organization as role models, and take cues from them about styles, colors, and accessories—from the color of suits, patterns of ties, dresses vs. suits, cotton handkerchiefs, watches, shoes. Emulate the look you aspire to.

Identification is critically important in selling; therefore, you should dress in a way that allows you to fit in with your colleagues, and that does not put off your customers. Regardless of how informal your customer base is, you should present yourself as a professional at all times. Avoid wearing anything that will distract or offend (big rings, clear nail polish on men, long long nails on women, noisy bracelets, etc.) your particular customers. Use your judgment in regard to what you wear, and always choose clothes that you feel comfortable in. While you should maintain a consistent image, your wardrobe should allow you to adapt to various situations. For example, when calling on a freewheeling company in the Silicon Valley, you probably will want to wear a tan suit instead of navy; or when invited to see a farm on a Saturday you might wear boots, corduroys or jeans. Since your appearance is important, when in doubt about dress, ask your manager or a customer about attire for an event or outing. It is also useful to observe dress norms particular to your own organization; see whether or not men wear jackets in the elevators.

Women (Some Additional Comments)

Women do not have the clear-cut guidelines in dress most men have. They actually have more leeway in colors and

45

styles. A woman's objective for dressing professionally is not to dress like a man but to keep on an *equal par with male counterparts* regarding *level of dress.* Just as a man would not wear a polo shirt and khaki pants during regular business hours, a woman should not dress in a casual fashion (polo shirt and skirt) for business. In general, suits, blouses with finished necklines, dresses, blazers and skirts, *closed* pumps, hose, and tailored accessories work best. Trust your judgment in dress and *make sure you are comfortable in what you wear.* Remember that your clothing can work for or against you, so don't wear clothing that will create a distraction. *When in doubt, don't!* If you have questions about the appropriateness of a pair of shoes (too high), a belt (too wide), a necklace (too showy or funky), or certain color combinations, do not wear them. In general, entry level women should pay special attention to this rule of thumb, but regardless of your level, it is important to have a role wardrobe that is professional, consistent, and comfortable.

Briefcases

Observe senior managers in your company for guidance in selecting briefcases, and so on. A conservative leather case in brown or black works well in most financial institution environments. Worn is fine, and in many environments preferred, but soiled is not. Keep the material inside your case organized so that you don't waste your time looking for papers and don't make your customer worry about your ability to organize yourself, let alone him or her. Since it is often necessary to carry cumbersome materials, you may also need a professional-looking carrying bag. Dirty canvas tote bags, jammed full and open at the top should not be used when you are with customers.

Women who carry handbags and briefcases often find

themselves juggling the two. Therefore, many women choose to carry a small handbag that slips into the briefcase during meetings, thereby keeping one arm free for shaking hands and so on.

ELEVATING CONTACT LEVEL

If you encounter resistance as you attempt to raise your level of customer contact, that is, from cash manager to treasurer or investment manager to senior portfolio manager, you can use a joint call with your midlevel manager or senior manager to help you move up a notch. A joint meeting in which you bring your senior officer and a senior level customer together is an effective way to raise the level of contact. A phrase such as "Ben, . . . our General Partner would like very much for us to meet with you and Jan . . . " will help you get to the senior without ruffling the feathers of your present contact.

Remember to debrief your manager, set a call *objective*, and decide on roles, introductions, action steps, and the like, *beforehand* to make the most of the meeting. It is *essential* for you to conclude the meeting with an action step in which you maintain the contact with the senior level or you will find yourself right back where you started! (See DECISION-MAKING UNIT and JOINT CALLING – PREPARATION.)

EMPATHY (RELATING)

If you can't empathize, you won't be successful in selling. Phrases that show your concern, such as "That must have been a *tough* situation," or "I'm sorry to hear that" when the customer reveals a problem or concern are essential in developing positive interpersonal relationships. Some salespeople who are normally empathetic are insensitive to their customer(s) because they are overly focused on their sales objective. Genuine empathy stems from caring about your customers and being prepared and willing to listen and *respond to what is on the customers' minds*, whether or not it is in your sales call plan.

Empathy is as important in telephone selling as it is in face-to-face. One young investment banker learned this the hard way when he basically ignored his customer's concern about his daughter's having just dropped out of college. Instead of showing empathy and realizing that this was not a good time to talk business, he said, "Don't worry, she's bright; she'll go back. What I'm calling about is . . . " Needless to say, that sale did not get very far. Empathy costs little and pays excellent dividends. It says, "I understand."

ENTERTAINMENT

By all means invite your important customers—current and prospective—to corporate or individual outings, meals, and so forth, but be aware of timing and protocol. Offering tickets to a show on the first call smacks too much of "buying the business" regardless of how genuine it is. When the timing is right and you are at the theater, at a game, on the green, or sailing, *don't hammer away at a specific product or deal.*

In social situations you are expected *to sell the value of your institution more than any specific product.* Use the opportunity to influence your customer's thinking about your organization; state that it is a great institution to be associated with because of "thus and such," and tactfully mention a specific opportunity. You can use a quick comment such as "What do you think of X stock?" and "Let's get together next week," to pave the way for the next business contact, or you can inject a business comment and then turn your attention back to the baseball game. You can also use situations such as driving home in the car as the time to compliment your customer's staff on their helpfulness.

The time you spend arranging the logistics of the social event can be an excellent second line of communication to the customer for tactfully reinforcing an idea or deal. An investment banker leveraged off his social contact in just this way—by using his eight calls to the customer to arrange an evening at the orchestra as an opportunity to bring up a particular deal and to finally sell it.

Entertainment is a great way to develop a closer relationship with your customers. It helps build a cushion that will protect you when something goes wrong (technical, operational problems),and can add to the enjoyment you derive from your job. This does not mean that socializing will make up for incompetency or lack of competitiveness, but the trust that goes along with a "good" relationship is a life saver when the inevitable problem occurs. Entertainment does not mean "Do this for me today, and I'll do this for you tomorrow," since building relationships is a long-term situation. Nevertheless, entertainment is a great way to help develop the relationship by helping you really get to know your customers.

Be on time for any event, but if your organization is hosting an activity be sure to arrive early, *before* the customers arrive. If your firm's invitation calls for cocktails at 6:00 P.M., you should arrive at least by 5:30 to lend a helping hand and be there to greet customers. A group of young brokers learned this the hard way when they arrived to find the president of the firm alone, greeting guests who arrived 15 minutes early.

Remember to follow up on the social contact. Don't think that entertainment will automatically lead to business because it will not. Customers expect you to come after business, not wait for it. (See DINING OUT.)

FEATURES/BENEFITS/NEEDS

When you discuss a product with a customer, remember to talk about features and *benefits*. Features, simply and clearly stated, tell what the service is and how it works. However, features alone are not enough. It is a product's benefits which have meaning to the customer. Features tell what the product does; benefits tell what it does *for the customer*, and what the customer will get as a result. Features give a product *credibility*; benefits give it *marketability*.

In analyzing your own selling approach, you may find that like many other salespeople you discuss features, features, and more features. There are numerous reasons why you may be doing this. Some of the most common reasons for feature-heavy selling include not knowing what the benefits are, thinking that benefit selling is too much like hard selling, not knowing which benefits are important to the customer, and assuming that the customer already knows what the benefits are and would resent repetition.

Regardless of the reasons, unless you *link* features with benefits you are using only *50 percent of the language of selling*. Even in situations in which you think the customer is aware of the benefits, you should state them anyway because reasonable repetition reinforces value and advances your ideas.

Feature/benefit selling should not be done in an awkward, self-conscious way such as "The feature is . . . and the benefit is . . . ," but rather in a personal, conversational way in which *features*, *benefits*, and *needs* (the customer's situation) are linked together: "John, you mentioned the *problem with getting paychecks* to your sales force covering the Northeast. We could have their *checks directly deposited to their own banks* . . . (feature). Thus you could be sure your sales-people *get their money on time* . . . and *eliminate the prob-lems you are having* with . . . (benefit). What do you think of . . . ?"

The skill of linking features and benefits does not seem to come naturally to many salespeople. You should practice us-ing phrases such as ". . . which means . . . ," ". . . so that . . . ," and "in this way you would . . . " to help you develop the habit of *bonding* features and benefits as you talk about your prod-ucts. The skill needs to be practiced, but it is well worth the effort because it will enable you to personalize how you talk about your product and services, and help you sell them.

FOLLOW-UP

The responsibility for follow-up after a sales call is always with you, the seller. Therefore, you should clarify what the next steps will be at the end of each call to move things along, and prepare yourself for the next step. At the end of the call you should clarify *who, when, where,* and *what.* As soon as possible after the call, write down or record all important information for your files, and mark follow-up dates on your calendar to ensure you follow up on commitments. If you tell a customer you will do X by Thursday, but you cannot meet the deadline, call *before* or on Thursday to keep the customer posted. After you make a sale, follow up with the customer to find out how things are working out. If the customer is satisfied you will reinforce his or her reason for selecting you, and if there is a problem you will have an opportunity to fix it. Follow-up letters are also a tool for relationship building. You can use them to thank the customer, to remind the customer about the next steps or commitments, or to reinforce ideas important to the customer. Follow-up skills separate top professionals from everyone else; therefore good follow-up habits will help you distinguish yourself from other less professional salespeople who lose track or lose interest.

FOLLOW-UP CALL REPORTS

Keep a *written record* of each customer contact whether the contact is *face-to-face* or by *telephone*. It is amazing how few salespeople write things down, and it is little wonder that so many sales opportunities are lost. You should develop a one-page customer contact sheet to help you keep a record of each contact, and use it to prepare for the next contact. Your contact sheet should note the name of the relationship, your contact(s)/functions, new information, needs, opportunities/ concerns, priorities, projections, results, agreements, follow-up steps, time frames, the person to contact next, who should be involved/apprised in your organization, materials to get ready, and last but not least, personal information such as "13-year-old daughter in state tennis tournament" or "upcoming scuba diving trip." Keeping such records will help you be more effective in your next contact.

This kind of recordkeeping, far from being time consuming, is a time-saver. Recordkeeping serves several important purposes: it allows you to *prepare* for the next contact so that you and your customer can benefit, enables you to plan, follow up, and fulfill commitments on time, and provides a *relationship history* to provide your customers with consistent, quality service. (See PREPARATION and TELEPHONE SELLING.)

"GIVE CREDIT BACK"

You can create a positive sales climate in which your customer's organization supports and lobbies for you. One important way to create this kind of situation is by "giving credit" to all customer contacts, from secretaries and operations people to senior executives who aid or support you in any way. It is at least as important to do this "backward" with support staff down the ladder as "forward" with senior management up the ladder. "John (treasurer), thank you for meeting with me. Ann (portfolio manager) was very helpful in preparing me for our meeting . . . . I really appreciated her . . . ." John will pass the compliment on to Ann. During a social outing this kind of professional compliment is a great way to mention the business relationship without getting into business. You should also remember to say, "Ann, thank you for the preparation and introduction to John." This positive reinforcement will help ensure continued support at all levels.

Even with very difficult customers, it is worth your while to find ways to "give credit back" for any ways in which they were helpful. For example, in a situation when an assistant does not convey a message properly, it could be to your advantage to suggest to the customer, "Perhaps I was not clear," to reduce confrontation and avoid making enemies.

Also do not forget to give credit back or acknowledge and *share credit* in your *own institution* with colleagues and specialists if you want their continued support and time.

HANDOUTS

Don't distribute materials during a face-to-face sales call or group presentation until you are ready to use them, or you will find yourself competing with your own handouts for your customer's attention. Customers will miss important ideas that you are presenting if they are flipping through brochures, proposals, or other handouts. Customers who do this are not trying to be rude. They probably feel obliged to look at what you give them. If a customer rushes ahead of you in looking at your presentation materials (you are on page 3 and he or she has flipped to page 10), you should pause, be quiet for a moment, and if there is something that is important to cover say, "Terry, there is something I'd like to cover for a moment on page 3." The fact that the customer is advancing at a faster pace than you are should cause you to at least question your own pace, and if appropriate make adjustments in your pacing, level of depth, or the perspective you are presenting. When a treasurer says, "Yes, I think I understand the basics. What . . . ?" and starts flipping through the proposal, you should *take the cue to move things along or possibly advance to your summary page.*

Whenever possible *personalize handouts* by highlighting and underlining certain areas, using a paper clip to indicate a particular page, or clipping your business card to the handout to point out to the customer how you think it applies to him or her.

Under all circumstances, make sure you have enough (extra) copies of the handouts for everyone attending the meeting, and make sure the handouts are crisp and error-free. If someone walks in late, pass material to the late-comer without disrupting the presentation. In preparing materials, check that the date is correct, all names and titles are correct, and that the *pages of your presentation material are numbered to facilitate your using and referring to them.*

HINGE/REFERRALS

A hinge refers to a point you share in common with a prospective or present customer. Sharing something in common often makes your contact more receptive to you and makes you more comfortable in initiating contact. The best hinge to warm up a "cold" call (call by telephone or in person on a prospect you do not know) is a *third-party referral* through which someone you and the customer know in common introduces or recommends you. Possibilities for third-party referrals include attorneys, CPAs, associations, and present customers. Most excellent salespeople have this "someone knows someone" attitude. Other kinds of hinges include *letters* sent in advance of a telephone contact, reference to *articles* which have appeared recently in the business press, or any new occurrence such as a promotion or change. Certainly the third-party referral is the best hinge in prospective situations, but any hinge, from an article about the company to a letter you sent to the customer, is better than going in completely cold. A comment such as "I'm Jim's banker (broker) and he suggested I call you" can do much to pave your way. One of the best ways to create a hinge is to ask for referrals from present customers. For example, you could say "Jim, I know that you have been pleased with . . . . Would any of your associates benefit from . . . ?" [See OPENING (GIVE BEFORE YOU GET).]

HOSTILE COMMENTS

A customer may say something you perceive as hostile, such as "You're really *socking* it to us with the terms," or "You're racking up the hours around here. I can hear the *meter ticking*." When you sense hostility or anger, it is important not to respond in a defensive way. Many salespeople react in a "defense mode" when they think they are under attack. While a defensive posture is crucial for combat (or flight), it isn't very helpful in most normal selling/business situations, since it is not the best environment for learning or discovering.

It will be very useful for you in potentially hostile sales situations to develop the ability to respond first in a "problem solving" mode so that you can discover if you are really being attacked. You can do this by *asking a nonhostile question* which will assist you in understanding the message the customer is trying to send. A nonhostile response such as "Well, I hope we are worth it. What do you think?" to a comment like "racking up the hours" will give the customer the opportunity to express what is really on his or her mind and let you understand if a problem really does exist or how serious it is. But more importantly it will enable you to resolve the problem. If you respond immediately in a defensive way you probably won't find out what is going on. By showing empathy and asking nonhostile questions, you will be able to create an environment in which concerns can be understood and resolved. In the "racking up the hours" example, the customer replied that he did think the consultants were worth it.

HUMOR

Humor can take the edge off a tense moment. A witty comment or a pun can relieve tension and help build rapport. You should be cautious, however, to make sure your humor does not offend the customer or reduce the seriousness of the business at hand. It is critical not to joke about something that is very important to the customer or about a sensitive matter. All racial, sexist, and ethnic jokes are potentially offensive and should be avoided.

"I"

Although you always represent your organization, there are times when the pronoun "I" is more effective than "the bank," or "our firm," or the royal "we." The word "I" shows personal ownership and accountability. Comments such as "*I've* given this thought and *I am looking at* . . . ," and "I think this is the time to make a move" are more likely to evoke attention and action from a customer. The semantics of "I" or "we" are not what matter. What does matter is that you are communicating that *you* take responsibility. Also when you are discussing a decision or problem, you will gain your customer's respect when you acknowledge accountability. By using the pronoun "I" and not "they" you can demonstrate that you assume accountability. In the long run customers will not respect you if you blame "operations," try to separate yourself from an area of the bank that is experiencing problems, or show any signs of disloyalty. Remember, institutions don't build relationships, cross-sell, or up-tier; individuals do. (See MISTAKES/FAUX PAS/ERRORS.)

INCREMENTAL SUMMARY

Don't confuse closing incrementally with an incremental summary. One does not replace the other. Of the two, closing incrementally is by far more valuable because it enables you to learn what the customer thinks about what you have said. For example, an incremental summary such as "I think that this letter of indemnity would protect you . . ." *will reaffirm your point of view.* However, closing incrementally (*question*) "How does the letter of indemnity designed to give you protection satisfy your concern . . . ?" will help you understand what the customer thinks and how satisfied he or she is. While your summaries are important, especially to help the customer focus and keep him or her on track, in the final analysis it's your customer's view, not yours, that sells.

Summaries do play an important role in wrapping things up while maintaining control. Therefore, when it is time to summarize, *you should be the one to do so* to reduce misunderstandings and to ensure that things are positioned from your understanding. A brief final summary should be made *right before* you ask for the business. The final summary should be short for impact, customer- and benefit-oriented, emphasizing "why" your institution is the one to choose. The summary should recap what was covered. It should not include any *new* information.

INTERRUPTING THE CUSTOMER

Never interrupt a customer! When you and your customer both begin to talk at the same time during a sales interview, it is *the customer who should be given the opportunity to speak.* *Stop talking and listen* when the customer speaks or is *about* to speak. You can do more selling by listening than talking. During a sales interview you should welcome and encourage customer comments, and create an environment in which the customer sells himself or herself. Remember, if you LISTEN to your customers they will tell you how to sell to them, and help you sell to them by "selling themselves." [See also LISTENING (NEON WORDS).]

INTRODUCTIONS ON FIRST CALLS

On a first call, whether with a prospect, a new assignment, or a reintroduction call, as you introduce yourself clearly state your full name, the name of your organization, and your role in the team (e.g., industry specialization), group, or division as these relate to potential value to the customer. Don't go into a lengthy dissertation on your organizational structure, but *briefly address the aspects of the organization that can add value* to the customer. You can talk for several minutes' or longer depending on the customer's interest. For example, "I'm with X, in the . . . group . . . . We . . . . I don't know how much you know about us. . . . May I take a minute to explain . . . ? We . . . to service this market."

Also, you should remember to have your business card conveniently at hand to present. Keep in mind the value of rapport building, and remember not to skim over the opening. [See BUSINESS CARDS, JOINT CALLING — INTRODUCTIONS, OPENING (GIVE BEFORE YOU GET), and RAPPORT.]

INVITATION TO YOUR
ORGANIZATION

Invite your customer to visit your organization and meet the people, particularly as a way to build confidence in operation-based products, to see facilities or new areas, to strengthen relationships, or to smooth out a relationship problem with a customer who is dissatisfied, feels slighted, or ignored. Tours, luncheons, seminars, invitations to participate in focus groups—all can be used to solidify and expand the customer's relationship. If customers are coming from out of town you should assist them with hotel arrangements, plan entertainment, and so forth. Remember to follow up on these events to gain maximum benefit from them.

JARGON

Avoid all financial jargon when you explain or discuss a product/service unless your experience with the customer indicates that it is appropriate (e.g., traders talking to traders). Terms such as DTCs, ZBAs, LPOs, IPOs, LBOs, Edge Offices, LIBOR, Butterfly Spread, agent, and the like, can confuse, intimidate, and annoy customers. (See CUSTOMER LEVEL OF KNOWLEDGE.)

JOINT CALLING—
INTRODUCTIONS

It is important to introduce specialists and other team members by briefly providing background on them and telling why they are there. The introduction can be made by you or your colleague, and should be used to establish credibility. It is important to plan how the introduction will be handled, and what, when, and who will do it.

Usually there are two introductions. The first one, a brief exchange of names, occurs quickly during the greeting, and the second, a fuller introduction, occurs as you begin the call or make the transition to the specialist. Simply saying to a customer, "I'd like to introduce you to Jack Smith from our Cash Management area," is not as effective as *telling the customer about Jack's background and the potential value to be gained from the meeting.* The introduction should briefly explain Jack's experience, background, how you work together, and how the team approach is designed to benefit the customer.

Prior to your bringing a specialist in to meet a customer, you can refer to the specialist by name ("Terry Sharp is in our Merchant Banking Group. She has . . . deal . . . I think . . .") to set the stage for him or her.

JOINT CALLING—PREPARATION

When preparing for joint calls with specialists, managers, or other colleagues, define roles and orchestrate how the interview will be handled by determining who will open, who will handle pricing, how introductions will be made, who will handle broad policy issues, and who will be responsible for the close, follow-up, and so forth. For example, a manager can handle broad bank policy issues, while the account manager deals with specific service or relationship items; or the account manager can open and introduce the specialist, turning the discussion over to him or her for the more in-depth presentation. During the presentation the team members should remain attentive and supportive, making comments that reinforce not only what the other teammates say, but also what the customer needs. After the specialist has completed his or her presentation, the account manager can make a final summarization of the key points and next steps.

It is very important to *decide* who will close at the joint call. It really doesn't matter who closes as long as the close occurs. Usually the member of your team responsible for the next step or follow-up should close to move things along. However, when the account manager passes the baton to a specialist, it is important in most situations for the account manager, as coordinator of the relationship, to stay involved, following up to make sure the customer is satisfied.

The *roles of all parties on your team must be clearly defined and agreed to prior to the sales call* so that you don't work at cross purposes or find yourselves in conflict, contradiction or disagreement with one another.

In joint call situations be sure to advise your customer that a colleague will be accompanying you, since you should not bring anyone unannounced. Also if you are arranging the joint call, be sure to qualify the lead so that you don't waste time for your customer, your colleague, and yourself. (See JOINT CALLING—INTRODUCTIONS, SALES TEAM, and SEATING.)

JOINT CALLING AS A TEACHING TOOL

Although joint calls can be *invaluable* for teaching entry-level or less experienced salespeople, the number of salespeople that can be taken on a particular call for teaching purposes should be limited to *one per customer* per call, and the customer should be thoughtfully selected.

During the introduction, the senior person should explain the new representative's presence by discussing the program, the team approach (improving response time or backup), and the new rep's role in the team. Managers should be careful not to refer to trainees or new people as "juniors," since this will make it more difficult for them to assume responsibilities with these customers in the future. Whenever feasible the managers should build in at least a small part of the sales call for the new rep so that he or she can begin to establish credibility as a part of the team.

LATE JOINER

When a third party in the customer's organization joins a sales call which is already in progress, you should make sure that a brief summary is made. If the customer does not summarize, or does so incorrectly/incompletely, *you should tactfully be the one to summarize. DON'T FORGET to ask a question or two, to identify the need or interest level* of the new party and to bring him or her into the discussion. This is critical since many late joiners are the *senior* people!

Remember, regardless of who the late joiner is, the late joiner's needs must also be identified. Frequently the late joiner may be less enthusiastic than you and your customer, and may even be resentful at having been *summoned* to participate in the meeting possibly without advance notice. In any case, a meeting which had been going well could *fall flat* if you do not bring the newcomer into the discussion by incorporating his or her needs. You can do this by having an *abbreviated second opening* in which you question the new party about areas of interest and concern. This must be done quickly and gracefully since you don't want to "lose" your initial customer during this catch-up/join-in phase. *You should also be sure to divide your attention evenly* (eye contact, questions, distribution of materials) *among all parties* during the meeting.

LAUNDRY LIST

Avoid presenting a "laundry list" of all the features and benefits of a particular service. *Focus on the features and benefits that relate to the customer's needs and situations.* Although it is necessary to make assumptions about what the customer is likely to be interested in, you should test your assumptions early in the call so that you can present product, specific product features, and benefits which relate to the customer's situation. (See FEATURES/BENEFITS/NEEDS.)

LISTENING (NEON WORDS)

Selling is often equated with talking, but successful salespeople know that listening is their *most important skill.* You may find that because you are so intent on selling and figuring out what you are going to say or formulating your next question, you fail to listen to your customers. But although listening to customers can be difficult at times, you cannot sell if you do not listen.

Some tips to help you *listen* throughout the sales interview are:

Keep eye contact

Listen with your body by keeping your posture erect

Face and look at the customer

Take notes at appropriate times

Here are tips to help you *use* what you hear:

Take mental or written note of *neon words* (words which are important to the customer)

Integrate these neon words into your responses and comments

Keep track of your talk/listen ratio ("one mouth, two ears" ratio)

Constructive listening means not only understanding but also *using* what the customer says. Paying attention and understanding what the customer says is step one of the listening process. Step two is incorporating what the customer says into your response. This second step is critical because it is your way of letting the customer know you understand. Your objective in incorporating your customer's words (neon words) is not to manipulate the customer or to make you sound like a parrot. Weaving into your presentation what the customer says to you will enable you to tailor (personalize) what you present to each customer. If you carefully watch an excellent salesperson at work, you will notice how he or she "naturally" integrates words and examples the customer has used. This communication technique really perks customers up because they, like all people, enjoy hearing about what is of interest to them. Integrating what the customer says and what is important to him or her into your product presentation will help you relate your product/services to your customer's specific situations.

By absorbing the customer's neon words, and using them as you describe your product capabilities (features and benefits), you can avoid sounding like you are making a "canned pitch." For example, if your customer says, "What I am looking for in my letters of credit are network, service, and price," you might say, "Yes, . . . our network . . . with your *suppliers* in *Rome* we could . . . to get the . . . to your headquarters." It is your ability to link your product features and benefits to your customer's buying criteria that will distinguish you from competitors and enable you to make customer-driven, not product-driven, presentations. The more you listen, the more you will understand your customer, and the more you can communicate that understanding, the more you will sell.

MISTAKES/FAUX PAS/ERRORS

As Albert Ellis, noted psychologist, teaches, "It's okay to make a mistake." Of course it is better to learn from your mistakes, take care not to repeat them, and prevent a continuous stream of errors due to a lack of preparation. However, the best thing to do in the face of what seems to you to be a glaring and "dumb" mistake is to honestly and nondefensively acknowledge it. An obvious mistake such as calling a customer by the wrong name during an introduction to senior management is a perfect opportunity to acknowledge that you are a fallible human and to let your natural self come through. You might say one-on-one to the customer, "John, earlier I introduced you incorrectly. I apologize. I had Tom on my mind. For the moment, I guess some wires crossed." This may even evoke a similar acknowledgment from the customer, who may say, "I understand. Names drive me crazy too . . . ." In any case, by acknowledging the mistake you will show the customer that you are human enough to err yet professional and confident enough to correct the error.

If your operations area makes a mistake, you should call the customer *before* he or she calls you. Don't say, *"They* messed up." Say something like, *"We* have a problem on this end . . . has happened. *I will . . . to correct it. I'm sorry* this happened, and we will work to correct it with . . . I will keep you posted and call you . . . ." By acknowledging problems or errors you will preserve your credibility and protect working relationships.

NEGATIVE PAST EXPERIENCE

It is important for you to have as much information as possible regarding any negative past experience a present or prospective customer may have had with your institution. For this reason it is ESSENTIAL that calling/contact records be kept up to date. Knowing about past problems will enable you to be the one to raise and *acknowledge* the problem *before* the prospect brings it up. When you do think it is appropriate to raise the point, acknowledge it in a calm, brief, nondefensive way. This will help establish your credibility, defuse the problem, and possibly prevent the problem from blocking future opportunities.

If you are aware of an important past problem when calling on a prospect, but do not acknowledge it, you may open yourself to attack and criticism from the customer and you may seriously damage your credibility in the prospect's eyes as well. Even if the customer does not bring it up, the past problem can block opportunities.

If you are caught unaware and a negative past experience is brought to your attention by the prospect or customer, show empathy, ask for details, take notes to indicate that you are seriously interested and plan to look into it, and *explain how the situation has changed*. For example, a prospect may say, "You turned me down six years ago. Why are you here now?" To this, you could respond, "I'm sorry to hear you had that experience with us. May I ask a little about the circumstances since I was not aware . . . ." After the customer gives you some details, you should explain how things have changed (hopefully they have). You would say, "With our expansion, we have made a commitment to this area (industry) as seen in our . . . *I hope today we can begin a dialogue to see how for the future we. . . ."* Unless you can resolve this kind of objection or obtain agreement to table it until you can look into the matter, you probably will not stand much of a chance with the prospect or customer. Of course, to reduce surprises you should *do your homework* before seeing the prospect or customer to find out what has transpired, who has called on your customers, or if your organization has ever had a relationship with or ever called on the prospect before.

NETWORKING IN YOUR CUSTOMER'S ORGANIZATION

Identify the gatekeepers, users, influencers, and economic decision-makers in your customer's organization and plan a strategy to reach them. By monitoring your customer's decision-making unit you can take advantage of many of the possible opportunities that exist. It is often necessary to find tactful ways to get to other decision-makers, particularly when you get stonewalled. One correspondent banker who was unsuccessful in selling to the "gatekeeper" closed a deal by going directly to the cash management department (user), circumventing operations.

One way to penetrate new accounts and maintain or expand relationships is to broaden the contacts you have with each relationship. You can ask your present contact to introduce you to other decision-makers and influencers in the organization and then do multilevel calling. By leveraging your point of contact, you can not only find additional opportunities but you can actually strengthen your total relationship with your present customer.

You can use a present contact to introduce a specialist from your organization by saying, "John, we have some excellent people in our merchant banking group. They are working with . . . (references) to . . . (benefit). Who in your company might be the person for them to see?" Also by finding out "who knows whom" you can use contacts outside your customer's organization who can help you influence your customer.

In many situations you can also use pressure points from your own institution by having one of your senior managers *tactfully* influence your customer or his or her manger. For example, the president of a bank called the CEO of a major client to praise a creative financing package that his own bank's team had suggested to the client, asking the CEO what he thought of the financing idea. The president directly asked for the business by saying, "We'd really like that piece of business." On another occasion, a bank president, after a luncheon in the company's executive dining room, asked if he could meet with an operations person for "a minute" and used the minute to discuss a large international letter of credit the company would soon require. The president expressed how much they'd like having it directed to them. In both situations, senior management influence worked!

Another excellent way to network your customer's organization is to initiate contact between technical counterparts. For example, one bank president said he always got other people in his bank involved. For example, he suggested that his head of bookkeeping take his customer's accounting staff to lunch. By establishing contacts like this he found that problems got short-circuited and that cross selling opportunities were uncovered.

It can be very beneficial to "attack" the customer at more than one level. Multilevel, multiarea contacts not only help you find and maximize opportunities today, but will help you develop a "depth" of contact that serves as insurance should your key contact leave his or her position tomorrow. (See DECISION-MAKING UNIT.)

NETWORKING IN YOUR OWN ORGANIZATION

The ability to influence your own institution and bring appropriate resources to your customers is *one of the most invaluable skills* you can develop.

There is absolutely no question that informal influence is important to getting things done *when you need them!* Thus, you should establish personal contacts and build personal credibility. When you call a colleague in a specialized group or in operations, for example, make a point to have met him or her personally and take a *second* for small talk before discussing your objective. ("Bill, this is John Harris. *How's it going today?* . . . Mr. Abbott called . . . I'd appreciate if you could . . . When . . .? *Thank you.*") Periodically make the request to see "Bill" and meet his coworkers face-to-face, not over the telephone. Remember, whether it is operations or product management, you need them. Show that you appreciate their output, empathize with their problems and respect them personally. They will be more likely to go to bat for you when you need them.

Unless you have your internal contacts in place, you won't be able to sell within your organization, whether it is to convince a specialist to add a bell or whistle, to have senior management dedicate a scarce resource to your priority customer, to get an exception on a policy issue, to sell a new idea to senior management, or to get a "rush" through word processing. (See CREDIBILITY and "GIVE CREDIT BACK".)

NEXT STEP

As the seller, follow-up activities are your responsibility. Therefore, you must ask questions and get agreement on the next step at the conclusion of each contact. Rather than leaving things open ("I'll call you within the next few weeks"), end each meeting with an agreed-on action step ("Would next Tuesday be convenient?" or "What day next week is convenient for you?"). When customers take control by saying "Let me get back to you," you can agree but add, "If I don't hear from you (both traveling, etc.), may I get back to you by the end of next week?" as a way to leave the door comfortably open for your following up. [See ASKING FOR THE BUSINESS (CLOSING) and FOLLOW-UP.]

NOTES

For one reason or another some managers tell their sales-people not to take notes during a sales call. Perhaps this is because note-taking has become a lost art. Actually, sensible note-taking can be an excellent sales tactic. Not only can it help you keep track of important details, but it can also help you control the sales interview. Times to take notes include taking note of figures or other details presented by the customer, writing down a name or a question that the customer wants you to follow up on, taking note of a customer complaint or anything you promise to follow up on. Jotting information down shows you are serious and intend to *follow through*. Depending on your relationship with the customer you can decide whether or not you need to ask permission before taking notes. *Under all circumstances you should be sensitive to when and how to take notes.* Do not take notes or even take out your pen when confidential, sensitive, or political subjects are discussed. Also do not take notes too early in the meeting and under no circumstances write down every detail. Only make note of key information such as key words and figures. In joint calls, generally only one team member should take notes at a time. Also, be sure to *remember to continue to make eye contact* as you jot down information and details.

Immediately or *as soon* as possible after the face-to-face call, organize and expand your notes so that you have the information you need to follow up and prepare for the next contact.

Note-taking can also be an excellent *negotiation* control tactic. By "making note" of a point, you can respond without committing. For example, you can say, "Yes, that's a point.

Let me make a note of that (without making a commitment). What other concerns do you have?" Taking notes will help you follow up in a professional and timely way. How and where you write down the information is important as well. A pad, not a scrap of paper, should be used since it looks more substantive and is less likely to get lost. As you take notes in a face-to-face interview, make sure that you do not doodle.

Remember to take notes when you are talking with customers over the *telephone*, to keep a record of details and of what you have committed to and to make note of customer needs and concerns. During each telephone call you should jot down *several* key ideas which you can refer to before your next contact. [See LISTENING (NEON WORDS).]

OBJECTIONS

Objections are opportunities to build your credibility and satisfy customer concerns. If you cannot resolve objections, you will not sell. Yet in spite of this, many salespeople are ineffective in approaching objections. They accept the objection at face value, they give up too soon, or they resort to contradicting or challenging the customer. None of these approaches can lead to real problem-solving.

When customers object they are in a negative mode. The best way to resolve an objection is to understand and reduce their negativity. You can do so by showing you are listening, concerned, and open to hearing what the customer has to say. Listening does not mean that you agree with what the customer says. It does show, however, that you accept the customer's right to his or her point of view and that you empathize with and want to understand the customer's perspective. If a customer says, "You are the highest priced in cash management in the area," rather than jump right in with a rebuttal, you can show empathy by repeating the objection with a comment like "I know you want to get the best price, and how important cost savings are to you with . . ." After you express *empathy*, ask yourself if you know enough about the objection to resolve it. Since most objections are general, you probably will have to get more information before you can address them appropriately. The empathy statement should help neutralize the situation and earn you the right to ask a question to narrow down the objections. For the cash management price objection you would ask, "May I ask what you are comparing us with in thinking we are the highest priced?"

Asking such questions will not only tell you enough about

the objection to approach it in the best possible way, but it will also get your customer involved in a dialogue for mutual problem-solving. Once you show the customer you are listening and that you are interested enough to get specifics, you can proceed toward resolving the objection. When you are confronted with an objection, look at it as an opportunity to understand and focus on the customer's concern and provide the customer with more information.

For example, when a customer says, "You are just too far away from us," you could use the four-step Objection Resolution Model.

Steps	Example
1. Show empathy by repeating the objection	"George, distance is, of course, a consideration." (Reframe it; respect the customer's right to his or her point of view)
2. Clarify by asking a question	"What specifically concerns you about our being headquartered in Boston?" (Find out what's *really* bothering the customer so you can address his or her *specific* concern—the issue that you *assume* concerns the customer probably does not!)
3. Present appropriate product/bank information by citing features and benefits that relate to the customer's concern	"Our L.A. office provides . . . and our . . . network . . . will ensure that you . . ." (Personalize your response by presenting relevant features and benefits)

4. Close incrementally by asking the customer if the concern is satisfied

"How does our office in L.A. . . . ?" (Check if the customer's objection is satisfied. *Don't assume that you have satisfied the objection if the customer listens quietly; get feedback)*

OBJECTIVES/FLEXIBILITY

Once you have done your homework and set sales call objectives, you have to be prepared to switch gears if the objective you set does not fit the customer's particular priority. While objectives are critical, *it is important not to be blinded* by them. In an effort to meet your own objectives, you should be careful not to ignore your customer's objectives. Therefore, you should test for agreement on agenda items early in the call. Setting objectives is a part of sales call planning, and *in the planning stage you should be highly disciplined*. But like all "best laid plans," you must be open and flexible enough to respond to new information or needs when they are identified. Although you should always have a game plan, you have to be able to scramble if you find a flaw in your plan or if an unanticipated need, opportunity, or situation arises. (See PREPARATION.)

OBJECTIVES FOR SALES CALLS

A sales call objective is to a salesperson what the finish line is to a marathon runner. Without it, it is difficult to know how you did or where you are. For every sales call you make you should have an *output* objective that is clear and measurable. Broad objectives such as "to move closer to the deal," or "to discuss the reorganization," or "to make the relationship more profitable" will not really help you measure your performance since they are not descriptive or measurable. You should set specific output objectives that specify *what you will see* and *when you will see it.*

You can translate a broad objective like "to move closer to the deal" to an output objective by asking yourself the question "What will I see to let me know that I have moved closer to the deal?" The output objective would look something like this: "To arrange for my senior vice-president and me to meet with the parent company and the other subsidiary within the next month." This sales call objective is measurable (either you and the senior vice-president go or you don't) and has a time frame. The broad objective, "to make the relationship more profitable," could likewise be converted to a sales call objective by specifying "to increase balances by X by the end of the quarter, or to collect X fees by that time frame." The advantage of output objectives is that they enable you to measure and evaluate your progress, performance, and results. As you write your objective(s) also keep the customer in mind, taking into consideration how each objective will benefit him or her.

OFFSETTING COMPETITORS

Of course the more competitive information you have prior to your sales interview, the easier it will be to offset the competition. Knowledge of what the competitors are doing will allow you to *ask questions and make comparisons in a professional way* that can strike at your competitor's weaknesses. While you should never downgrade the competition, your role is to maximize the strengths of your deal/organization. For example, if you have a strong international department you can ask, "How are they going to handle your foreign items . . . ? Will that be through a correspondent?" and then point out the efficiency and specific cost savings of going with your institution. When you do not have specific competitive information, you can ask your customer about competitors' products or services so that you can help customers compare value.

The key in offsetting the competition is to make comparisons, taking in the "all in price" and total value. How you do this is as important or more important than what you say. Do not make derogatory comments and avoid showing signs of being intimidated when a competitor is mentioned. One of the best protections against the competition is to believe in yourself and "create competition for yourself." A comment such as "Yes, I'm familiar with X's . . . . What . . . ? Most of our clients, such as . . . , find that since we can do both sides of the transaction and since we do . . . percent . . ." will communicate your belief in yourself and spark in your customer confidence and desire to do business with you. [See SIDE-BY-SIDE (BETTER OFFER), TOTAL OFFER, and COMPETITIVE INFORMATION FROM CUSTOMERS.]

OPENING (GIVE BEFORE YOU GET)

Avoid the temptation to *rush* through your opening. Use the opening to begin to build rapport and help focus the customer's attention on the sales interview. Remember, of course, to take cues from the customer to determine how much time you have to open, particularly how much time you can spend on rapport building. An effective opening usually includes the greeting/introduction, rapport building (nonbusiness or nonsales call related), summary of the previous contact or how you got to see the prospect, purpose of the call and potential benefit to the customer, and general agreement on the purpose of the call. Whether it takes two minutes or 20 minutes, all of this should and can be accomplished in the opening! The rule in sales is "give before you get," and the opening is a perfect time to give so that you earn the right to find out about your customer's situation and priorities. The opening is an opportunity to begin to build trust and reduce tension; therefore, it should not be glossed over. (See INTRODUCTIONS ON FIRST CALLS.)

PLAYERS AT THE NEXT MEETING

It is important to know about and help select the people who will be at the next meeting/presentation. By asking the customer, "Is there anyone you'd like to have attend the meeting or presentation?" you can indirectly initiate invitations to key influencers and decision-makers who should be at the meeting. Remember to ask questions such as "So that I can prepare, who will be at the meeting . . . ?" and "How much time will we have?" Once you identify who will participate in the next meeting, you will be able to prepare for it. *Find out as much information about the other customers as possible from your contact. Find out about their backgrounds and orientation so that you can satisfy their needs and eliminate as many surprises as possible.* Knowing customer buying criteria is essential, particularly when there will be several customers at one time. You may also find it very helpful to meet with the individuals one-on-one prior to the meeting to identify their particular needs and line up their support.

POINT OF VIEW (CUSTOMER'S PERSPECTIVE)

Discuss features of a product from the customer's perspective, *not your organization's*. Rather than saying "Our target market is over $60,000," it is more *customer-driven* to say "Our experience is that customers like you with $60,000 . . . benefit most, since . . . ." Or, rather than saying "Your company fits well into our structure . . . ," it is better to say "We are organized so that . . . for your . . . ."

POST-CALL SELF-CRITIQUE

You are not really selling if you don't ask yourself, "*How did it go?*" at the conclusion of each sales call. Don't rely simply on a gut feeling; use specific criteria as a checklist. Ask yourself:

Did I establish and maintain rapport?

Did I identify needs?

Did I uncover more than surface needs?

Did I know my services?

Did I question?

Did I link features and benefits?

Did I tie the products to customer's needs?

Did I meet the buying criteria of all decision-makers and influencers?

Did I listen?

Did I resolve objections?

Did I ask for the business?

Did I achieve my objective?

This kind of self-analysis will help you evaluate results and improve performance. Remember, as one top performing investment banker says, "Feedback is the breakfast of champions" and self-feedback, like the model for a self-portrait, is always available. As you give yourself feedback, remember to give yourself feedback on both strengths and areas for improvement.

PREPARATION

The cost of a sales call, the pressure of aggressive competitors, and respect for your customer's time make it inexcusable for you to go unprepared to a sales call. Preparation—reading files, doing research, meeting with product managers, setting a strategy, and setting an objective—is essential if you are to be effective and maximize results. An investment banker discovered this the hard way *after* receiving a long-awaited call-back from the CEO of a top priority prospect. He spent his precious ten minutes on the telephone discussing the same product that he covered five weeks earlier. Although the customer listened politely, neither he nor the salesman benefited from the call. If the salesman had reviewed his call report (in this case it was available on a screen at his desk!), and checked for needs before making the full presentation, he could have used his and the customer's time more advantageously.

Preparation will help you maximize your time. For example, if you review your prospect's portfolio before the call and discern that the prospect is a value buyer, you can prepare information to support that investment philosophy. Before each call prepare your call strategy and objective. Unless you do this you are likely to waste time and dollars.

PRETTY/HANDSOME

Tactfully ignore comments such as "It's nice to see a pretty face" or "I suppose your children have your good looks" from a customer or prospect. Give the customer the benefit of the doubt. He or she may be trying to be friendly and make you feel welcome, rather than trying to throw you off guard or make an inappropriate overture. Ignoring a comment that might be inappropriate is usually the best way to discourage it. Such comments are given with the hopes of getting a response. Totally ignoring them seems to be the best way to stop them. You can direct the conversation to business quickly by saying, "Thank you, I'm happy to meet with you to discuss . . . ." "Thank you" is polite, yet though it may seem to reflect back to the compliment, by attaching it to your business purpose, you can launch into the call and move the discussion toward business.

PRICE OBJECTIONS

Don't cave in when a customer says to you, "X tells me that you are the highest priced in this area." Don't give in by saying, "We take balances," "We discount," "I agree," "We'll lower it," "No, we are not," or "You get what you pay for." Rather, empathize with the customer's concern for price, and then nondefensively ask questions to find out the basis for the statement. *You really can't answer this objection unless you find out exactly what you are being compared to* because price is relative. Being able to ask questions in a positive, confident way will help you withstand price pressure from manipulative customers and will give you the information you need to justify and preserve your price.

When price is being discussed, *it is time to get specific.* It is your job to help the customer understand what a cost differential translates to, and to make sure the customer connects cost with value. An advertising executive who has never lost an account because of price is an expert at this. Although his space is 30 percent higher than his two top competitors, he demonstrates with statistics that his publication reaches a wider audience by 30 percent. It is the isolating of the amount of money and the value to the customer which enable him to preserve price and win and keep accounts. *Before you meet with* the customer you should *prepare* cost comparison figures in advance whenever possible to be ready to spell out specific savings and value for the customer.

Only after you find out what you are being compared to can you compare price and value. When a customer says, "X is less expensive," you can say, "I can see you'd want the best deal. May I ask what their price is? What is included in their offer?" Similarly, when a customer gives you a figure that is unacceptable to you, you should ask, "May I ask how you arrived at that?" to gain insight into the customer's thinking and assist you in resolving the objection. Once you and the customer understand specifically what is being compared/considered, you can begin to resolve the objection by making a cost/value comparison and selling your *total offer*. Also, remember after you state your price, be silent or you are likely to talk yourself into making the first concession—the first to speak after price is stated is often the first to fold. [See OBJECTIONS, TOTAL OFFER, and SIDE-BY-SIDE (BETTER OFFER).]

PRODUCT KNOWLEDGE

You should know fundamental sales information on all products important to your customer base. Unless you have a direct lead to a customer who wants to discuss one particular product, you will have to "scan" for needs and opportunities as you set the appointment and during the sales interview itself.

Product knowledge is essential for transactional or relationship selling. Successfully initiating (not merely responding to) a sales opportunity requires that you know fundamental in-depth information such as key features and benefits, product differentiation, probing questions, needs which are satisfied by the product, common objections, target market, qualifying criteria, basic operations and implementation information, pricing parameters, competitive information, action steps, the market, and how the product is sold. Product knowledge is the foundation of selling and is fundamental to relationship building. Differentiating your products is more often achieved by what *you* know about your products and *how* you present the information than by the actual technical differences among products. (See CROSS-SELLING.)

QUESTIONS

Questioning is a critical sales skill. Effective questioning will help you uncover deeper levels of needs and understand what the customer's real priorities, requirements, and constraints are. How and when you ask questions is as important as what you ask. The following techniques will help you develop your questioning skills for more effective selling.

Gap Questions

Ask questions that will help you and the customer analyze the present situation and determine how things could be improved. These questions will expose the *gap* between what the customer is doing and what the customer could be doing. In this gap lie your areas of opportunity. The time to ask questions which reveal the "gap" is early in the sales call, right after the opening. For example, a successful investment banker says he approaches all prospects in fundamentally the same way. After he introduces himself and his firm he says, ". . . as you know we are a large firm. We provide many financial services. I have to know what you do, so as not to waste your time . . . ." Then he listens and/or asks questions. This approach is *very* effective, since most customers love to talk about how they operate, how they are structured, and what is important to them. This investment banker says, "I can't sell until I understand how the customer thinks"—great advice for all salespeople. (See CUSTOMER NEEDS.)

Incorporating Feedback with Questions

Make a point of mixing questions with feedback to the customer so that you don't sound like a prosecuting attorney. It is important to give as well as take, especially when you question. By alternating questions with feedback you will encourage the customer to talk more. Grilling the customer with back-to-back questions, three or four in a row, with no intermittent feedback from you will eventually close off communications.

Grilling (questions with no intermittent feedback):

SALESPERSON: When are you planning to begin selling abroad?

CUSTOMER: We . . . trade show in France.

SALESPERSON: What kind of interest was there from potential buyers at the trade show?

CUSTOMER: A number . . . inquired.

SALESPERSON: Whom do you see as buyers?

CUSTOMER: Small companies that . . . we don't know.

SALESPERSON: What terms will you use in selling to them?

Healthy dialogue (questions with intermittent feedback):

SALESPERSON: Whom do you see as buyers?

CUSTOMER: Small companies that . . . we don't know, so . . . .

SALESPERSON: *Yes, I can see your concern about payment. Given that you don't know these small companies and . . . ,* what terms will you use in selling them?

In the first group of questions, the salesperson "grilled" the customer and paid no attention to the relationship level, but in the second set, questions were mixed with feedback to create a balanced dialogue.

Open-ended Questions

Rather than ask questions that elicit one-word, yes or no responses, you can ask *how* and use the five W's of journalism (*who, when, what, where,* and *why*) in questions like "What problem . . . due to volume?" and "How would being able to monitor . . . be helpful?" to *develop a meaningful dialogue with your customers and gather important information about the customer.*

Posing Sensitive Questions

In selling situations, it is important not to offend customers with questions that make them defensive. Sometimes one word can ruin an otherwise good question. For example, one account executive asked, "What *problems* are you finding in implementing the plan?" Instead of discussing the plan, the customer defended how well things were going and "clammed up" about details. It would have been more effective to ask, "What kind of things are you seeing in implementing the plan?" Look at and listen to your customers, and back off from or reposition questions that seem to offend customers. Asking questions even on sensitive matters is critical in selling. While you may have to ask hard questions on sensitive matters, you should do so in a tactful way to protect the relationship and person and still get the information you need. Whenever possible ask sensitive questions one-on-one, since there is less potential for embarrassment and more chance for openness.

Prefacing Questions

Prefacing can make both you and your customer feel more comfortable with the questions you ask. Prefacing involves beginning (or ending) the question with an explanation of *why the question is being asked*. By doing this, you can get customers to "join you" in answering the question. For example, "To determine . . . I'd like to ask how much you are planning to invest . . . ?"

Silence after Asking a Question

After you have asked a question, be quiet and give the customer a chance to answer. Unfortunately you may have developed the habit of answering your own questions, suggesting several multiple choice answers, or expounding on the question with a lengthy explanation. Answering your own question often stems from a feeling of discomfort with asking questions, or not being able to withstand the silence or pause between the question and the answer. Prefacing and trading should help make you more comfortable asking questions.

Trading Questions

Trading is a skill in which you preface a question with information. Basically you are setting a pattern in which you and your customer exchange information: "We have seen . . . in the industry. What are you seeing with . . . ?"

QUESTIONS—ONE AT A TIME

Ask *one* question at a time. When you string a group of questions together, important questions will go unanswered either because you and the customer will simply forget some of them or the customer will be selective in which ones he or she will answer. One banker asked, "From where do you import?" "What is the size of your . . . ?" and "How do you . . . ?" all in one breath. Needless to say two of the three questions went unanswered.

RAINBOW SELLING

If you like your customers you will most probably enjoy and succeed in your job. The greater the spectrum of customers you like (with whom you can identify and who can identify with you) and genuinely show you like, the greater the spectrum of customers you will be able to get to know, understand, and ultimately sell to.

RAISING OBJECTIONS YOURSELF

You should be the one to raise an objection that your experience says is likely to become a stumbling block later in the sale *even if the customer does not bring it up.* For example, in discussing trust or investment products you should inquire about attorneys and financial advisors with the objective of meeting them, even if the prospective customer does not mention them. These influencers will probably have a role in the final decision and it is important that you gain their endorsement.

RAPPORT

Never underestimate the importance of building rapport with prospective and present customers. Identification between buyer and seller is a critical factor in sales and rapport building *early* in the interview. It allows you and your customer to get to know one another. Of course, although rapport building is especially important when opening, the positive interpersonal communication should continue through the call/relationship.

The initial rapport stage, often called icebreaking (talking about topics of mutual interest such as sports, foliage, even the weather), is more than just a nicety. It is the overture that prepares the customer and you for the sales call and establishes a common connection. Rapport building is most effective when it is genuine and specific to the customer based on observation (open your eyes and look around) or homework. A salesperson with good rapport building skills would observe and comment on a photograph of the Labrador retriever (a salesperson with a little luck will also have a Lab!). One very successful senior executive revealed that the secret of getting to him was on the wall of his office, and an account representative who did not tune into it "didn't really stand much of a chance!"

Before the meeting you should go out of your way to find out as much as you can about the customer's background, interests, affiliations, and position, whether from people in your own institution, homework, board members, or secretaries, and use this information in a tactful and appropriate manner. It is important to take a cue from the customer about how much time is available for the rapport building phase. Too many salespeople mistakenly assume that they should "get down to business" immediately and do not take the time to establish rapport. On the other hand, some salespeople mistakenly extend rapport building when the customer is clearly eager to get to business. The point is to take the opportunity to build rapport and get to know the customer, unless the customer clearly signals "get down to business—now." Use a few moments to your advantage: Get to know the customer and let him or her get to know you.

Rapport goes beyond icebreaking. In the more developed stage, it evolves into the relationship that is the key to doing business—the person-to-person bond. [See ENTERTAINMENT, DINING OUT, OPENING (GIVE BEFORE YOU GET), and RELATING.]

RECOVERY

During a sales interview when you sense your call is not going well (i.e., customer stops looking at you), *do not* continue as if the customer were in tune with you and the meeting were going well. The first step in remedying the situation is to trust the internal signal or intuition which alerted you to the possible problem and to calmly test your hypothesis. This is the time to stay calm, *think*, and *ask questions* to determine what is important to the customer, or *go back to a nonthreatening subject, or even go back to building rapport* (yes, go back to rapport building). For example, a saleswoman felt from what the customer said and how he said it, that he was giving a courtesy interview and had no intention of buying. The customer said, "We are very satisfied with X, which was here when I started the job . . . ." The saleswoman sensed relationship tension. Rather than ask about X or talk about her product she responded, "Oh, well, how long have you been here?" and decided to try to get to know more about the customer rather than press a product discussion. The saleswoman learned to her surprise that the customer had had a negative past experience with her organization in his previous job. After they talked about the problem the customer accepted an invitation to lunch. The meeting prompted the customer to ask for a proposal that was later accepted and implemented.

The main thing to remember is not to hammer at your service or drone on in the same vein when you feel you are losing your customer. If you think the sales call is not going well, it probably is not. You can recoup if you pause, think, change the pace, highlight key points, ask questions, or get the customer to talk about his or her perspective or what is important

to him or her. The key is to trust yourself. If you sense something is wrong, try a new tack.

REFERENCES/CASES/EXAMPLES

References, cases, and examples are credibility builders. Particularly with a new or skeptical customer, always be prepared to present references, examples, and case histories of satisfied customers. This will help you build customer confidence. Of course you should have the permission of the customer to use him or her as a reference. You will find that most customers are *flattered* when asked.

In choosing references, be absolutely certain about the kind of reference you get. Do not overuse one customer, and use your judgment in determining who should contact whom (levels, industry, or whatever criteria you think are important). Remember to thank the customers who serve as references for their time and endorsement.

As much as possible prepare examples in advance, especially examples specific to the company, to show how a particular service would benefit the customer. For example, you might prepare figures to demonstrate to the customer how much he or she would save by leasing a fleet of trucks as compared to the current plan.

REFLECTION/PAUSE

It has been said that "dumb is smart." Think twice before rattling off answers *too* quickly so that they do not seem glib, canned, or slick. Without being dramatic you can pause to show that you are thinking or that a question is thought-provoking. While you are doing this, use the time to think about what you are going to say! (See SILENCE.)

RELATING

Your ability to relate to customers on a personal basis is often a major factor in getting and expanding business. Therefore, during every sales interview, it is very helpful for you to be conscious of the two levels on which you are operating: the relationship (person-to-person) level and the sales (sales/problem solving) level. If you focus exclusively on the sale and ignore the "person" part, your sale may never get off the ground.

As a case in point, during a sales interview with a prospective customer, the customer described to a banker for ten minutes how well his toy company was doing. He boasted about his growth in annual sales and his expanded sales force. He talked about his plans for expansion. When the customer stopped talking the banker responded with the question, "With the expansion, how satisfied are you that your present credit lines are adequate? Will you be looking for an increase?" A critique of this response would give the banker high marks on the task side since his sales question was excellent. But it would give him lower marks on the relationship side. The banker did not take the opportunity to begin an interpersonal relationship that would set the foundation for the business relationship. An excellent salesperson would reinforce this customer openness with a genuine compliment such as "You're doing very well. That sounds great. You must be doing something right to show that growth. What do you attribute it to? . . . You mentioned the expansion. How well will your present lines accommodate the growth you are planning?"

Because the banker was so focused on his task, he became blinded to the customer as an individual, and missed an opportunity to connect with the customer. Of course, all relating comments should be genuine and appropriate for the individual and situation. By responding to the person as well as the opportunity, you can establish a relationship conducive to business. Some salespeople are excellent on the people side but neglect the sales side and never do get around to doing business. While other salespeople are technically sound, they fail to establish the line of trust and empathy needed for a solid relationship. The most effective salespeople develop a balance and blend of the personal and business. (See RAPPORT.)

SALES TEAM

In situations in which you are the overall account manager, you should, whenever possible, personally introduce your product specialists and participate in the call since you know the customer. During the sales call it is important for you and the specialist to demonstrate a coordinated team effort. This takes pre-call planning. If the specialist is to be the one to follow up, it makes sense for him or her to make the closing arrangements on the product discussion. Nevertheless, you as the relationship manager should be the one to *open* and *close* the meeting and then recap next steps.

As the overall account manager, you will probably serve as "point person" for *bringing in* or coordinating all of the specialists and resources of your institution to the customer. You should make sure the customer knows how the team works and whom to call. This can be accomplished by comments such as "Remember, call me at any time if there are any problems," or "Joan is the specialist, and if you'd like we can give you her direct line to . . . ," or "Our investment people . . . will call you each day . . . ."

Team members who support one another and present a coordinated approach are in the best position to maximize opportunities and serve the customer. A solid team approach can be effective in competitive presentations, in preliminary joint calls, and even when team members are calling individually. For example, an account manager could support the cash management specialists and demonstrate a team approach with a comment like "I was speaking with Jack Smith yesterday and he mentioned he would be meeting with you next Tuesday to . . . . I've worked with Jack. His approach . . . our technology . . . ." This team approach is far more professional and helpful to the customer than a statement such as "I hope Jack Smith isn't bothering you." By lobbying for and supporting one another (gathering information, building confidence), team members can expand and protect relationships. (See JOINT CALLING—INTRODUCTION and JOINT CALLING—PREPARATION.)

SEATING

Be aware of seating possibilities as you enter a customer's office, conference room, or conversation area. Select the seat/seating arrangement that will work best for you. Your aim should be to establish an advocate configuration, right angles to one another, rather than an adversarial situation, head-on—locking horns position, sitting directly across from one another. By taking the right angle chair or opting for a conversation area when you have the choice, you can eliminate physical barriers and create an environment that is more conducive to working together. Usually you cannot move your customer's furniture (although most effective salespeople will move an office chair forward or to the side, or ask to change their seating arrangement if it is uncomfortable—glaring sun, etc.), but you *can* make sure you make the most of the set-up that exists. You can position your own colleague in the spot that is "adversarial" to you as a way to prevent your customer from taking this spot and to give you eye contact with your teammate. In group meetings it is a good idea for you and your colleagues to mix in with the customer group, rather than set up an "us against them" configuration. Also, in planning seating arrangements, make sure you have easy eye contact and access to your teammate(s).

SECRETARIES

Secretaries are people too. They are your best communication channel to your customers. Therefore, it is essential for you to develop positive relationships with them. Do this by *asking for and using their names* and treating them with consideration and respect. Be sure to get their names right. Do they prefer to go by their first names, to be called Mrs., Ms., Miss, Mr.? In addition, try to pick up on their styles (curt vs. chatty), which usually fit in with the personality of their employers. Secretaries can often make or break you, so engage them as allies. Small courtesies such as saying "Thank you," "Hello, how have you been?" can help you develop relationships with them. It may also be appropriate to make gestures of appreciation such as a box of candy or a birthday card. Taking the time to get to know a secretary helped one investment banker discover an important piece of information about board ties. [See TELEPHONE (GETTING THROUGH SECRETARIES).]

SECRETARIES/ADMINISTRATIVE ASSISTANTS AS INFLUENCERS

Assistants often function as buffers between decision-makers and salespeople. These individuals may not have decision-making authority, but they often exert significant influence. You should be confident and friendly when you speak with them, whether face-to-face or over the telephone. When you telephone a prospective customer and the administrator intercepts the call, you should state your first and last name and your company's name, and ask to speak with the customer. When the assistant asks the nature of the call, state in concise and general terms the reason for your call, for example, "I'm calling about an investment opportunity." Never insult him or her by implying that the call is too complex or important for him or her to understand or handle. *Do not be condescending or impatient in these situations.* If you are put on hold, wait patiently. When you leave a message, spell your name and state your number. Solicit the assistant's help by asking when would be a convenient time *for you to call back.*

Ask for the assistant's name (jot it down near your prospect's name) and use the name during the call and when you follow up. Assistants are particularly important in prospecting since they often control the appointment book, and they can be an excellent source of information. For example, you could say, "Karen, I know Mr. . . . is really busy. Can I ask you something about your company? Do you do exporting? . . ." You can use this information to fact find and then prepare for the next contact. Remember to say "Thank you." The key here is to show respect and regard so that the assistant becomes an ally who will get you and your message to the customer.

SELLING TO A GROUP

Selling to a group of several customers at one time can be more difficult than one-on-one selling since in a group you are confronted with diverse needs and multiple customers. When you find that your presentation will be to several customers (decision-makers or influencers), find out as much as possible about the individuals who will attend the meeting, including their orientation, experience, and their role in the decision-making process *before* meeting with them as a group. Whenever possible, meet with them one-on-one prior to the group meeting to establish rapport and identify each individual's needs and motivations, and to forestall potential problems. When individual meetings are not possible, be sure to find out as much as possible about each participant from your liaison.

This kind of initial preparation paid off for one banker who was preparing for a second appointment with the president of a large commercial real estate firm and his sales force. When the banker inquired about the makeup of the sales force and asked about the top producers and their bank preferences, she discovered that the top producer of the firm had had a negative experience with her bank which had cost him an important deal. By doing some homework and speaking with this agent about the problem *prior* to the group meeting, she was able to smooth things out and eliminate future problems.

Multiple customers translate to multiple needs; it is very important to identify each customer's buying criteria and to address all of these during your presentation. In addition to coping with a number of customers and multiple needs, you must also pay special attention to your delivery skills, since projecting yourself to a group is somewhat different and often more difficult than a one-on-one situation. Such things as the arrangement of the room and clearing away any signs of other presentations or clutter (get there early), preparation and use of visuals, the ability to *keep eye contact with all members of the group*, and the quick, orderly distribution and use of materials—all must be managed.

It is extremely important to be on time for group presentations. While of course it is also very important to be on time for one-on-one calls, you should *never* be late for group meetings, because the participants are usually away from their own offices and the waste of time becomes glaringly obvious and uncomfortable. If you find that you will be late (traffic or air connection, etc.) telephone the customer as soon as you can get to a telephone. (See HANDOUTS, INTRODUCTIONS ON FIRST CALLS, PLAYERS AT THE NEXT MEETING and SEATING.)

SERVICES VERSUS PRODUCTS

Think about your capabilities as products but *discuss them as services*, emphasizing what they can do for the customer. Rather than saying, "One product that might help is coupon collection," it is better to present what the product can do for the customer. "Based on this, we can provide . . . (give feature and benefit)." When a customer expresses a need such as "freeing four people overwhelmed by paperwork," you should discuss features and benefits of your service that will reduce clerical work and free the four people for other tasks. You certainly can refer to the particular service by name but make sure your focus is on what it can do for the customer. (See JARGON.)

SIDE-BY-SIDE (BETTER OFFER)

Always remember that almost *no packages/deals* are identical. Therefore, when a customer says that he or she has another/better offer (price), it is essential that you and the customer look at the offers *side-by-side*. A comment like "Since there are a number of different factors that could influence the pricing, can we look at what is included in . . . as a way to compare and evaluate . . . ?" helped a salesperson offset what at first glance looked like a lower offer from a competitor. After he and the customer looked at and compared total offers, isolated the dollar differences and then factored in the balance requirements, the salesperson demonstrated to the customer substantial overall savings with his offer. This salesperson consulted with his customer and was able to meet the customer's needs and increase profits for his own organization by making a total cost/value comparison. (See PRICE OBJECTIONS and TOTAL OFFER.)

SIDING WITH THE CUSTOMER AGAINST YOUR ORGANIZATION

When you have to decline a request that your customer has made, you may be tempted to side with the customer against your own organization, or to place the blame on someone else in your organization (the credit committee, product specialists, management), or to say outright that you don't agree with the policy/decision. While it is perfectly legitimate for you to tell the customer that you "really went to bat" for him or her, you should never denigrate your own organization. It may seem expedient to "join forces" with the customer, particularly in situations in which you truly do not support your organization's decision, but you will find that in the long run, siding with your customer against your organization *will backfire* on you by damaging your credibility and weakening your position. While you may not champion the final decision, you should stand by your organization's position from the broader perspective. While lawyers, for example, can be used to a certain extent to deflect objections on technical points and reduce some tension, in principle you should support your organization's policies and decisions. The balance between serving the customer and protecting your organization is a delicate one, but one should not be served at the other's expense.

It may also be tempting to commiserate with a customer who expresses "sympathy" about a situation your organization is going through, such as a merger or bad press. Again it is self-defeating to "confide" in the customer and confirm how terrible things are. You should turn this into an opportunity to support your institution by thanking the customer for the concern but immediately pointing out the positive side:

"With a merger, we now have a new investment instrument available to you which will . . . ." (See "I.")

SILENCE

There are several times in the course of the selling process when silence is an effective strategy. Among them are: after you've asked a question (so that the customer can answer); when a customer says something outrageous (so you can give him or her the time and opportunity to reconsider it); when the customer is not paying attention (your silence will be noticed); when you need a minute to think; or, as a negotiation strategy for preserving price (since it is said that the first person to speak after a price is quoted will be the first person to fold).

Silence provides thinking room. The sales interview does not have to be a continuous babble. However, when obvious pauses occur during a sales call (not a negotiation in which silence is a very important tactic), it is your job to fill them.

SMOKE SCREEN OBJECTIONS

Smoke screen objections are objections that customers use to mask their real concerns. Typical smoke screen objections like *"Let me think about it"* are given by customers in lieu of their real concerns. They are used to avoid having to make a commitment or disclosing information.

Use the four-step Objection Resolution Model (see OB-JECTIONS) to find out if the objection is real or if it is a smoke screen. By testing (questioning) the objection, you can discover what is behind it. You can ask, "We've discussed . . . (benefits and points of agreement) . . . . What specifics do you want to consider? Perhaps I can shed some further light on them while I'm here." Your objective should be to unearth the customer's real concerns *while you are there* so that you can address them.

Even classic smoke screen objections such as the one mentioned earlier must be tested to find out what is behind them or if they are real. You can probably be sure that they are smoke screens if the customer is unable to defend or support the objection in depth, or offers a series of unrelated objections one after another (because there is no real depth to support any one).

Customers fabricate smoke screen objections for countless reasons ranging from not wanting to offend you, to deliberately wanting to mislead you, to wanting to protect themselves. In all cases, you should ask questions to get specific information to find out if the objection is real and/or what the underlying objection is.

Under no circumstances should you make the customer uncomfortable or defensive, so it is important to know when to back off. Nonetheless, always *make a second effort* — don't take the objection at face value. If you communicate that you are trying to be helpful, you will have a good chance of finding out what is really bothering the customer and of addressing/satisfying the real concern.

START-UP TIME

Ask about your customer's time frame *before* committing to your delivery or turnaround time. When a customer asks, *"How fast could you act on this?"* or *"When can we begin?"* you should respond by asking, *"When would you need it?"* In this way you can try to accommodate the customer's needs, rather than suggest a time frame that is inconvenient or unacceptable to him or her. The time frame you give might make you less attractive than a competitor or cause you to disqualify yourself in the customer's mind without your even being aware of it. When you must give a time frame without knowing the customer's requirements or preferences, be sure to ask how it fits in with his or her schedule. When the customer does not ask about start-up time, you should inquire about the customer's start-up requirements or decision time.

When the customer's time frame and yours do not match, find out more about his or her time pressures. Perhaps the customer *can accept the service in stages.* Look for ways to satisfy your customer's needs in a timely fashion, and be sure to deliver as much or more than you promised on time!

Above all, be realistic and do not promise what you cannot deliver. Do not unnecessarily delay start-up time, since this can cost you the deal. Take special customer situations into consideration and work with your team to improve turnaround and start-up time to meet your customer's needs whenever possible.

TABLE IT

In certain sales situations, you may need to table topics or issues in order to maintain control and to progress in the sale. You should table *new* topics, that is, subjects that the customer unexpectedly raises during a discussion on a particular subject (unless it is part of a package). *Usually* new needs or interests can be acknowledged and tabled temporarily until there is some *closure on the subject at hand, but this must be done in a tactful, sensitive way* so that you do not offend the customer.

Unless you can skillfully table topics, you may find yourself being bounced from one topic to another with no resolution or closure on anything. Of course you should use your judgment and common sense to determine if the topic raised by the customer warrants immediate attention, or if it can be tabled without offending the customer or missing a better/ more important opportunity. When the new topic is of greater priority or interest to the customer, you should switch to the new topic deliberately by mapping out the change in course. You could say, "Yes, let's discuss that now. We can get back to X in . . . ." *In this way you can maintain control and set a game plan for where the customer and you are going.*

When it is appropriate to table a topic, be tactful. Say, "*Yes*, Don, that's a good point I'd like us to spend some time on. Can we hold that for a few minutes and then give it attention?" Under no circumstances should you ever say, "*No*, let's get to that later," or "*No*, let's finish this."

Another time to table a subject is when a specific point is raised prematurely in the discussion, before the necessary groundwork has been laid. Some customers will jump ahead of you in your presentation and bring up a point which really cannot be covered until some more basic information is discussed. This is especially important when customers ask about *price* before you really know what they want/need and they understand what you can do. When customers say, "Just tell me the terms (price) before anything else," don't fall for the trap. Wait until you understand needs and the customer understands value. Again, never say, "No, I need to know . . . ." Rather, say, "*Yes*. So that we can discuss price, let me get the details. How much . . . ? What . . . ?"

Although knowing how to table topics that are not integral to the subject at hand is important in moving the sale forward, there are situations when it is not appropriate to table a subject. Such situations include, for one, comments on inquiries injected by a senior officer. *The seniority level of the customer who introduces a particular subject is a major determinant in whether or not something can get tabled.* For example, when a CEO says, "What happened to X?" you should address X *immediately* even if it is only to say you'll look into it and get back to the CEO. Another is when a customer has an objection which "interrupts" your presentation. There may be a temptation to say, "Well, let me just finish this first." When a customer has an objection that you can address on the spot, it is important to respond to it or you could lose the customer.

In all situations, when you do table a subject, you *must* remember to get back to it. A comment such as "Leslie, you mentioned your concern about cost earlier, . . . Now that we have the figures, I think if we look at them and . . ." show the customer you are listening and tuned into his or her needs. (See CONTROL.)

TELEPHONE (GETTING THROUGH SECRETARIES)

It can be difficult to reach a prospective customer because of a protective secretary or administrative assistant. But you can usually get through if you follow these tips: Make an ally of the secretary by being polite, ask and use the secretary's name, ask for his or her help ("Can you check Mr. Wilson's book?" "When shall I call back?"), and treat the secretary as an intelligent person. Your level of confidence is also a factor in getting through. Avoid a tone of belligerence or impatience, but don't sound tentative either. You may say something like "John Smith for Harry Tims, is he there?" An assumption tone and a positive choice of words can often help you get through.

You can also try calling before 9:00 A.M., after 5:00 P.M., or at noon when customers are likely to answer their own phones, or on Friday afternoons when managers are apt to keep their calendars free and are more likely to take your calls. You may decide to send a letter prior to the telephone call and refer to the letter (hinge) as a way to reach the customer. Your success with the telephone is directly proportionate to your persistence, persuasion, and politeness. Therefore, don't get discouraged, and always remember to say thank you. (See SECRETARIES/ADMINISTRATIVE ASSISTANTS AS INFLUENCERS and TELEPHONE APPOINTMENTS.)

TELEPHONE APPOINTMENTS

Present Customers

When telephoning a present customer to arrange an appointment, you can go into more depth to ensure that the agenda you are planning for the call is appropriate. Prepare for this call by making a checklist for call objective, assumptions, questions, decision-makers, logistics, and other information you need to prepare for the call. (See TELEPHONE SELLING.)

Prospects

When you telephone a prospective customer to set an appointment, do not lose track of your objective, which is to get an appointment. Don't be lured into trying to make the sale over the telephone. Prospects may say, "Tell me now . . ." and so on; however, it is usually impossible for the telephone to substitute for the face-to-face call you are trying to make.

When the objective of the telephone call is to get an appointment with a prospect, limit your call to just that. The format of the appointment telephone call should include a greeting, an introduction of yourself and your organization, hinge, potential benefit to the prospect, request for appointment, and confirmation of date, time, and place. Be prepared for the call with names and other relevant information. Take notes during the call to help you prepare for the appointment.

When prospects resist giving you the appointment, you should *repeat* the prospect's objection to show you are listening and are sensitive to the situation. Also repeat the potential benefit of the meeting. Don't hesitate to *restate* what you have already said when asking again for the appointment, *but this time suggest a limited time frame of 15 to 30 minutes*: "I'll be in the area . . . opportunity to meet each other, begin a dialogue, and determine if it would be appropriate to set a full appointment." This 15-minute tactic "because I'll be in the area" gets excellent results. When you do meet with the customer, honor your time commitment. (See HINGE/REFER-RALS.)

TELEPHONE: "EXTRA" CALL

The hardest thing to do is make that extra telephone call — the call that doesn't get returned, or the call to the unpleasant customer, or the call that has not produced any business yet. While it is essential to know when to stop — as an insurance salesman phrased it, "Know when you have a China egg" (a China egg is an egg that won't hatch) — it is too easy to give up too soon. Question yourself if you hear yourself saying, "I don't want to be a pest," or "He's too miserable to call." It may be that you are missing a good business opportunity because you don't want to go through the unpleasant experience of calling and being rejected. A better attitude is to look at the situation as an experience and to depersonalize it. Say to yourself, "What would I do if the opportunity were the same but the prospect were X, a prospect I feel comfortable calling?" Recognize that this unpleasant customer is probably unpleasant to everyone, and if you stick with him or her you may be one of the few left to compete.

Certainly you don't have to take abuse, and there is a point in each business in which prospects get deleted (at least temporarily), but it is very useful to question your own motives to make sure you are not missing good opportunities. One investment banker waited six months to call a prospect who was very angry with him and his firm. But after several more months of calls to give industry as well as other information, the investment banker was able to sieze a large merger intermediary opportunity.

TELEPHONE NURTURING

Use the telephone to solidify the relationship with a customer. Even if you are not following up on a specific item or purpose, you should use the telephone to nurture the relationship. You can do this by having a several-minute-or-so conversation with your customer about topical subjects such as earnings, a trend in the industry, a competitor ("What did you think about what X company did?"), or a "Hello, how are you?" or a call to extend a holiday greeting. While your antenna should always be up for opportunities, telephone calls with the purpose of keeping contact to nurture and cultivate the relationship are as important as face-to-face sales calls.

TELEPHONE SELLING

The telephone can be an excellent sales tool. However, there are inherent problems with selling on the telephone.

You usually cannot sell complex products to new customers over the telephone

You are apt to make errors or quick concessions because of the tendency to rush on the telephone

You may find it more difficult to build rapport or pick up on cues, since there is no opportunity to read body language or establish eye contact

You may be at a disadvantage with customers who call you if you are unprepared

You may encounter more rudeness on the telephone, since customers/prospects are more likely to say no or be impolite on the telephone, particularly if they have not met you

This last point creates the greatest problem with selling over the telephone, making many salespeople uncomfortable about calling customers they do not know to arrange an appointment or to sell. However, you should approach the telephone as a business tool with both limitations and *advantages*. If you keep your objectives realistic and if you are prepared for more rejection than you may be accustomed to in face-to-face selling, you won't be threatened by the telephone. Learning to use the telephone is very important because of the tremendous opportunities to generate new business by reaching a wide market or to upgrade and strengthen present business.

The following tips can help you to be more comfortable using the telephone to sell:

Look on it as an opportunity to learn and grow

Set a *block* of time aside and concentrate on the task

Set an objective (action step) for each call prior to making the call (refer to your last contact sheet *before* making the call!)

Be prepared with the information and files you will need; organize your desk (checklist, calculator, computations in advance)

Keep telephone contact sheets (time of call, contact or noncontact)

Take notes of key points (five or six) such as needs, concerns, follow-up arrangements, and the time to call back

Use the customer's/prospect's full name (Mr./Ms. unless you know the customer)

Be courteous

Ask if the customer has time to talk (if not find out when would be a good time to call)

Ask if the customer has gotten the information you sent and has it handy to refer to (if you had sent materials in advance)

Present benefits early

If rejected once, always ask again; don't hesitate to repeat your ideas using the same or different words

Have an upbeat, pleasant voice

Remember your customer can't see you and that you must verbalize your body language (your smile can't be seen)

Smile as you speak; it relaxes your throat and helps you sound confident and positive

Listen to the customer. Try to pick up on everything. Read between the lines since you don't have the advantage of a face-to-face call. If the customer is up, be up; if the customer is down, be empathetic but don't be down

If the customer calls you and you are not fully prepared, say you will call the customer back

Follow up on the opportunities/interest you generate

Say thank you and mean it regardless of the outcome

Remember the telephone is a business tool and don't take it personally

If you are new to telephone selling, write out your opening and key comments, and practice to help build your confidence and comfort level.

TESTING ASSUMPTIONS

As you prepare for sales interviews, you will make assumptions about the customer's needs, present mode of operation, attitudes, future plans, and the like. Assumptions are educated guesses, and they should not be confused with what the actual situation is. Recognize that your assumptions, while they are an essential part of planning, will not always be on the mark and may very well be completely wrong. Therefore, you should be prepared to test your assumptions *before* acting on them and proposing your ideas. By testing your assumptions, using questions to understand and expand on needs, you can refine your approach. Unless you test assumptions, you may spend valuable sales time covering topics of little or no interest to the customer or covering the right topic from the wrong perspective. (See "WHAT DO YOU HAVE FOR ME TODAY?")

THANK YOU/COURTESY

Make the words "thank you" and "please" a part of your sales vocabulary. Show appreciation for the business and time your customer has given to you; remember to thank the customer for the letter of credit business, and for his or her time ("I appreciate your meeting with me today to . . . "). Take the time to send a hand-written note to congratulate a customer for a situation that affects him or her personally, such as a promotion. Also, when a customer compliments you or your organization ("You're first class."), say thank you ("Thank you, it's nice to hear that.") as a way to reinforce the positive feelings the customer has about your organization. Whenever you ask for anything say "Please" and when you get it say "Thank you."

TOTAL OFFER

Studies show that customers have a difficult time distinguishing one product from another. What, then, causes them to buy from one seller over another? Certainly price is not the only factor. The total offer concept refers to the sum total of why a customer makes a choice to buy a particular service from one organization rather than from another. Price is a part of the total offer, but only a part. *You as the salesperson, and your ability to sell the total value of your institution, are factors that can differentiate your organization.* On a day-to-day level organizations don't sell; people do! If you do not understand and use your total offer, you will have a difficult time differentiating your institution and selling yourself and your total value.

Each financial organization has its own total offer which includes such things as network (whether it is worldwide or branches), quality of service, industry expertise, length of relationship, knowledge of the customer, technology, staying power in a market, innovation, personal attention, the quality and dedication of the salesperson assigned to the relationship, and most importantly, the ability of the salesperson to differentiate his or her products based on knowledge of all of the above.

While customers can generally be classified as either relationship-oriented or transaction/price-oriented, the number of situations in which price *alone* is the deciding factor is far fewer than many salespeople imagine. Often when price appears to be the sole deciding factor, there can be a hidden opportunity to offset price with something equally important to the customer. In fact, while there are strictly transactional deals, many customers are transaction-oriented only because the salesperson fails to use total value and the relationship. As you sell your services, don't think of them as commodities. Most financial services *can be differentiated* whether it be through technical product differences, or the uniqueness of an institution itself, a salesperson, or a sales team. Remember that *you* differentiate your capabilities by presenting to your customers a total offer—all the value and benefits of dealing with *you* and *your organization*. If you can't differentiate your products you are at a terrible disadvantage.

TURNOVER (CHANGE OF ACCOUNT MANAGER)

Recognize the impact that a change of account manager can have on a customer relationship. Relationships build confidence, and change triggers insecurity. If you understand this you will understand why customers need reassurance when an account manager is changed. If you are involved in a situation in which there is turnover, take steps to make the transition a smooth and, if at all possible, a slow one.

Ideally the transition should be made gradually by bringing the new salesperson onto the team while the team member is still there. When a gradual transition or introduction is not possible, a manager should become involved by introducing the new account representative. This demonstrates continuity and provides an opportunity to express the institution's commitment to and confidence in its new representative. When the new representative is inexperienced the manager should stress the team approach and the manager's role in the management of the relationship. If the new salesperson has extensive experience, the manager should emphasize it by detailing that experience. By paving the way, the manager can accelerate rapport and credibility, and smooth the transition. In any situation customers should not have to unnecessarily waste time educating new representatives.

In June 1984, a highly profitable private banking as well as corporate client ended a 50-year relationship with a major money center bank because, as he told his new banker who had been courting him for three years, "They didn't tell me they were changing my account officer." With him went his son's account. This is an extreme, but true, situation—and one that could have easily been avoided.

As the new account manager you should also be prepared to answer questions like, "What happened to Bill?" If there was a problem, you should not go into the "gory" details with the customer. You should be brief, nonjudgmental, and professional. Customers usually do not want all the details, and even if they do you should not provide them. When you, as the new account manager, are confronted with an objection about excessive turnover, you should use the Objection Resolution Model. (See OBJECTIONS.)

You can say, "I am aware that there have been three account officers over the past year and certainly understand your concern. I want to assure you I have done my homework, but before going any further, I'd like to know *if anything has fallen between the cracks because of the changes.*" With this approach you can relate to the customer and determine if there is a serious problem. You could then explain the new team concept, your assignment, your commitment, your manager's role, or whatever else is in place to address the turnover problem.

Remember, relationships are most vulnerable when account managers are changed, even when the change is handled well. This is the time to give a reasonable and honest expression of your commitment. It is also a time to be overly prepared and attentive to the relationship to ensure that another institution doesn't wedge its way in. Reassurance is key! Communication is vital. However, if the shoe is on the other foot, this is an opportunity for you to take business away from a competitor!

UNDERSTATEMENT

It is *better to understate potential benefits* to customers with the words "possibly" or "may" when you are *introducing* an idea or service early in an interview. You should *avoid exaggerated claims at all times, but especially early in a discussion.* Rather than saying, "We have a fantastic system for you . . . balance requirements," it is more effective (and believable) to say, "I think we can eliminate those problems through . . . so that you have information . . . ." Of course, this does not mean that you should not be enthusiastic about your products and confident of your capabilities.

VOICE PROJECTION

Speak clearly and confidently during the sales interview. Relax and don't forget to breathe deeply and regularly. Voice projection and intonation are important factors in conveying self-confidence, establishing and maintaining control, and *sparking excitement in your customers* during sales interviews. Women should be especially aware of the importance of voice projection and intonation to make sure they are not speaking too softly, thereby undermining their ability to project confidence and authority.

"WHAT DO YOU HAVE FOR ME TODAY?"

If you try to answer the question "What do you have for me today?" *before* you know how the customer thinks or what the customer needs, you will probably lose your opportunity to sell anything. As in the case of any assumption, unless you are very lucky, you won't address the "right" subject or you will find yourself approaching the "right" subject from the "wrong" perspective. Once again, the rule in selling is "Give before you get." Therefore, in response to the question "What do you have for me today?" you can give some background on your firm and the basic ideas you had in preparing for the call, but before answering the question you must say something like "Before I tell you all the . . . *to help me focus could you tell me . . . ?*" That same principle holds true for customers who ask, "What is your investment philosophy?" While customers may ask this, it is likely that they want to tell you their philosophy.

Of course, once the customer shares information with you, you had better have something to present that responds to his or her interest, or the customer will feel as though he or she has wasted a good deal of time and will be very reluctant to spend more time with you in the future. As one treasurer puts it, "I'll see any banker . . . once!" (See CUSTOMER NEEDS.)

YOUNG/INEXPERIENCED

When a customer says, "Frankly, you seem too young to really know my business," you should discuss the collective experience of your team, your direct manager, and your senior manager. You can also mention previous experience, experience in the organization, your background and your role in the team. *Most importantly, you should be thoroughly prepared for the meeting so that you can demonstrate your knowledge of the customer, industry, and so on.* For example, "I appreciate your frankness and understand your concern with quality . . . I've spent a good deal of time with . . . on your file . . . ." The key is to demonstrate your confidence based on preparation and commitment to working on the account.

Some customers may exert pressure on you if they perceive that you are new or inexperienced. Remember that you do not have to disclose your exact level of experience and should not unless you are pressed to do so. If directly asked, "How long have you been with . . . ," give an *honest but general answer* ("several months" rather than "nine weeks"). If the issue of authority comes up, remember *no one has unlimited authority,* so discuss your team approach and your ability to use your understanding of the company *to represent the customer fully to your management.* In all situations be prepared, and remember that you are not expected to have all of the answers or to make commitments on the spot. Don't try to answer questions out of your depth, or be pushed into making premature commitments that you cannot carry out.

Younger salespeople often can hold their own and build rapport with customers in their own age group but become intimidated by customers with more experience, status, or

power. To combat this it is important to be thoroughly prepared for calls, not only with technical background but also
with personal background on each customer, such as school,
interests, and affiliations. This information can be used, with
sensitivity and tact, to help the new salesperson feel more
comfortable and to develop a free-flowing dialogue and establish rapport. [See CREDIBILITY, OPENING (GIVE BE-
FORE YOU GET).]

"Z"

"Z" stands for the zillion other challenges that lie beyond the 101 tips addressed in this book. The bad news is that no salesperson ever has *every* piece of the sales puzzle. The good news is that you don't have to have *every* piece to sell successfully. You need only a good grasp of the basic pieces and the ability to apply the basics in a myriad of unique situations.

The 101 tips don't address 101 different sales problems. They address examples of sales problems. While there are an infinite number of such examples, there are really only a handful of sales problems—problems you can handle!

The key sales problems are:

Inability to relate

Inability to question

Inability to listen

Inability to integrate

Inability to check with the customer

Fortunately, there are five key solutions to these problems:

Being able to *relate* to customers by demonstrating empathy and caring

Knowing how to ask *questions* to find facts, expand needs, and help customers self-discover

Knowing how to *listen* in an attentive, intelligent, and responsive manner

Knowing how to *integrate* products and services with the

customer's situation and needs, to show how the customer will benefit

Remembering to *check* with the customer to gain feedback *throughout* and *at the end* (close) of the sale

Relating, questioning, listening, integrating, and checking are five skills that you can develop and refine. You can use these skills over and over and over again to solve sales problems and turn potential traps into opportunities. While you may use the skills in different sequences, in different patterns, and to different degrees, they are the essence of every interaction with a customer. They help you make the sales process work and hold the puzzle together.

These 101 tips will keep growing and disappearing. That is why I need to hear from you — the dedicated sales professional — about your personal challenges and discoveries. Please send your tips to me in care of my publisher so that we can all benefit from them in the next edition. I thank you on behalf of my own sales team and all of my colleagues in sales who *ask for the business every day.*

DATE DUE

OCT 5 '87			
DEC 0 9 '89			